INTERIOR DESIGN
PLANNING TO
SUCCEED

**A CONCISE GUIDE
WITH BEFORE-AND-AFTER
ILLUSTRATIONS
THROUGHOUT**

images
Publishing

Published in Australia in 2020 by
The Images Publishing Group Pty Ltd
ABN 89 059 734 431

Offices

Melbourne
6 Bastow Place
Mulgrave, Victoria 3170
Australia
Tel: +61 3 9561 5544

New York
6 West 18th Street 4B
New York, NY 10011
United States
Tel: +1 212 645 1111

Shanghai
6F, Building C, 838 Guangji Road
Hongkou District, Shanghai 200434
China
Tel: +86 021 31260822

books@imagespublishing.com
www.imagespublishing.com

Copyright © The Images Publishing Group Pty Ltd 2020
The Images Publishing Group Reference Number: 1560

A catalogue record for this
book is available from the
National Library of Australia

Title: Interior Design: Planning to Succeed
ISBN: 9781864708547

Printed by Everbest Printing Investment Limited, in Hong Kong/China

IMAGES has included on its website a page for special notices in relation to this and its other publications. Please visit www.imagespublishing.com

···· Contents ····

INNOVATION AS DESIGN DRIVER

"I have always believed in the power of space to transform—the banal into the poetic, the everyday into the sublime. My work seeks to create such spaces by redefining and distilling the elements of Place, Ritual, and Perception to their core—I term this approach Essentialism."

Where it all starts

For interior design, I think the best way is to question where the inherent potential in contemporary design lies, and then disturb the ways in which it is created or perceived, redefining the world around us in relevant and innovative ways, project by project. This, we declare, is real change—not change for the sake of novelty. Fortified with these aspirations, we begin each distinct project anew by seeking to do two things: to draw deeply from the context surrounding each project, and also to dream freely so that we might transcend mere reality and convention. Each project should endeavor to be delightfully surprising yet relevant, distinctly local but still globally appealing.

Combining the traditional and the modern

A key question we ask is how to innovate yet remain rooted in culture and location. Our overall approach is to begin with traditional roots and elements, and combine it with contemporary modern concepts.

A good example is The Prestige Hotel (2019), an independent bespoke 162-room luxury hotel that best evokes the natural urban beauty of Malaysia's Penang province's historic core. With its modern-day interpretation of Victorian design, it welcomes the urbane traveler to a contemporized and magical quasi-colonial universe. Located within the UNESCO World Heritage Site of George Town, set among the beautiful and intricate nineteenth-century English colonial buildings, the hotel has fabulously comfortable rooms, a great all-day restaurant, a rooftop pool for sunset cocktails, and a gym to work out in.

Using design narrative to make the design holistic

We believe it is important for a hotel to have a narrative expressed through its spatial experience, art, and design, from beginning to end. It makes the experience more memorable for the traveler. The Prestige Hotel is a modern interpretation of Victorian-era interior design layered with the local botany. In addition, we added elements of visual surprise through notions of illusion as design devices to animate spaces, also taking cues from the movie *The Prestige*, featuring the illusory art of magic, also set in the Victorian era.

Innovating the genre: to excite, immerse, and persuade

Not confined to the hotel typology alone, we are also thrilled to have opportunities to innovate in other genres, such as our latest retail project, Durasport, located in Moshe Safdie's iconic Jewel Changi Airport. In a mature market such as Singapore where online shopping is prevalent and there is no shortage of established multilabel sports stores, we had to ask ourselves this question when approached by our client to create a sports retail brand and its flagship store: "How do we make a brick and mortar sports store relevant in the twenty-first century?"

To draw foot traffic for any new-to-market brand, the storefront design has to excite. Conceived to be more than a typical retail frontage with large display windows, Durasport's façade is instead designed to appear as if in dynamic motion, conveying a sense of active, ultra-high performance sporting activities.

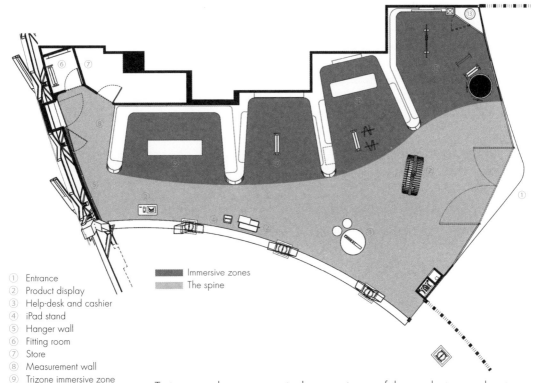

1. Entrance
2. Product display
3. Help-desk and cashier
4. iPad stand
5. Hanger wall
6. Fitting room
7. Store
8. Measurement wall
9. Trizone immersive zone
10. Climb immersive zone
11. Arctic immersive zone
12. Cycle immersive zone
13. Window display

Immersive zones
The spine

To immerse the customers in the experience of the product, we educate them and subsequently provide a related hands-on-experience. Highly customized and detailed display units illustrate the uniqueness of each item by showing how the item is "dissected," as with the use of an x-ray view of the components that make up the finished product, or by offering the customer the chance to put the item to the test.

Building on this, distinctively designed hands-on experiential zones allow customers to sample and test the sportswear or equipment. Aided by machines that simulate the activity they were designed for, this provides customers with a visceral experience to cap off their knowledge of the product and works to convince them as to how this item will help to improve their game.

High-grade stainless steel is used in a disciplined and cohesive manner as the primary spatial material, which is an intentional reference to the typical laboratory R&D environment. Specially designed to showcase Durasport's varied merchandise across four key sports, the customized display system allows for extended flexibility across the product and size range. Shelves, racks, or holders clip in and out of notched display walls and incorporate an integrated LED lighting system.

Durasport's entrance, interior layout, and materiality are all designed to excite and provide a fully immersive experience for the consumer, the discerning ultra-performance athlete.

Conclusion: innovation as a differentiating factor

I firmly believe that consumers can't be clumped into a singular entity. There are different subcultures and each desires different things. I believe the design industry will continue to spawn more niche interests, and each hotel or retail store needs to have its own differentiating factor in order to attract increasingly sophisticated global consumers. The key for designers is to continually innovate in order to create and curate new and authentic experiences for consumers.

Colin Seah, Founder-Director
Ministry of Design

Targeting the ultra-performance athlete, Durasport is the first in Singapore to feature the Freedom Climber, a non-motorized rotating climbing wall *(opposite bottom left)* so shoppers can test their climbing shoes without height risks. Adapting an X-symbol to represent the catalyst at the beginning of lab experiments *(page 10)*, Durasport's entrance beckons, using two open arrows at its doorway to invite the shopper to enter within. *Opposite bottom left and right:* Durasport is engaging in performance-driven retail, aiming to excite, immerse, and persuade athletes to "up their game."

Case Studies

The Ministry

Location / London, United Kingdom
Completion / 2018
Area / 50,902 square feet (4,729 square meters)

Client / Ministry of Sound
Design / Squire and Partners
Photography / James Jones

Squire and Partners is an architecture and design practice with experience spanning four decades, earning it an international reputation for architecture informed by the history and culture of where it is placed. Its award-winning portfolio includes masterplans, private and affordable residential spaces, workspace, retail, education, and public buildings for some of the world's leading developers. In addition, the practice has a series of dedicated teams for model making, computer-generated imaging, illustration, and graphics, and an established interior-design department that has created a number of bespoke product ranges.

○ **The space**

The Ministry is a social workspace and private members' club for those working in the creative industries, housed in a former Victorian printworks in Southwark, London. When designing the internal spaces, an important part of the brief was to combine the creative, social, and networking aspects of a members' club with dynamic workspace for up to 850 people from sectors including music, film, arts, fashion, and technology. The aim was not just to offer a place to do business, but to provide an environment for a convivial and creative way of life.

Desirable, practical working floors alongside generous social spaces were created to be as suited to morning coffee and lunch meetings as evening networking and social events. The brief looked for the design to create a set of spaces that could adapt for an evolving series of uses.

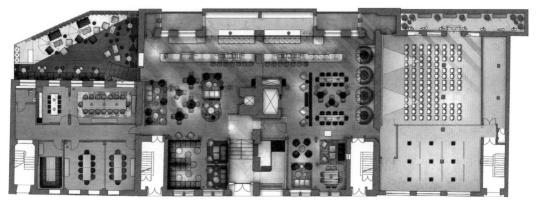

First-floor plan

This meant that the layout of the spaces was very carefully considered. Beyond the entrance and reception area, located at the center of the building, the entire first floor is designed as a generous social space with areas for eating and drinking. The bar and social spaces are designed to seamlessly change their function with different modes from morning to night, as well as throughout the week and seasonally.

○ **The flow**

When planning the layout of the first floor, the design was constrained by both the existing structure of the building—which divides the plan neatly into four—and the desire to locate the bar/restaurant at its center. A central spine running through the floor plan was therefore maintained during the design process, which provides direct access from it to all of the separate spaces.

A clear route from the entrance through to the bar/restaurant is defined, without the need to pass through any workspace. At the center of the plan and directly ahead of the entrance, lift cores provide access to the working floors above.

Within the open setting of the restaurant, four circular curtained booths offer more intimate spaces, and a new opening at the end of the lounge was made to create an urban garden with an outside bar and fire pit, which can be serviced by staff easily from the back-of-house areas.

The two areas on either side of the first floor's "social heart" space have distinct functions. The space to the right of the plan is used for events,

where curtains are used to split the space to suit different occasions (for example, one side operates as a pre-function area before guests move through to the other) and has its own external terrace. The additional terrace can be serviced directly from back-of-house areas without the need for staff to cross the central space, and means that occupants are not required to cut through to the main garden. On the opposite side, to the left of the plan, a set of meeting and private dining suites has been created, with the lounge used as a waiting area before entering the group of spaces.

On each of the upper working floors, a social space at the center of the plan surrounding the lift cores includes a tea point, lounge, informal meeting space, and a printer point, encouraging interaction between the different tenants on the floor. Phone booths offer an enclosed space for when total privacy is needed, and small meeting rooms at the edge of the social space are available for anyone to use.

○ Dividing the space

Curtains and screens are used to create temporary partitions between different areas on the first floor, creating a level of adaptability that, together with freestanding furniture, enables the plan to be highly flexible and space to be used in multiple ways.

The social space at the center of the first-floor plan is conceived as two halves, with the restaurant on one side and the lounge on the other. Although the 72-foot (22-meter) bar spans the length of this central space, puncturing through an existing wall, the restaurant

Section

(Before)

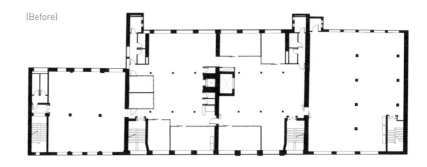

(After)

Second-floor plan

(Before)

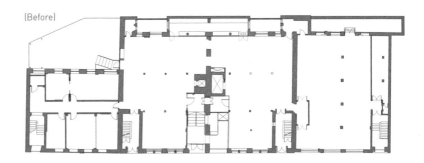

(After)

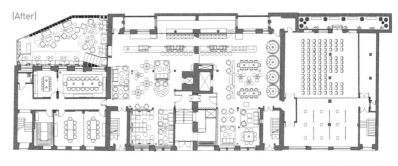

First-floor plan

and lounge can be divided using a curtain to enable two functions to take place at once.

Dining suites can be separated into two meeting rooms via a screen, or can be opened up into one boardroom. The suites can work much like the spaces in a house: with the kitchen kept separate while staff prepare food, or opened up to the dining space.

On the workspace levels, a "super track"—similar to a bulkhead or downstand beam—was created, and runs along the length of each upper floor to provide future flexibility by enabling partitions to be installed or removed, according to the requirements and growth of the businesses using the workspace.

The working floors contain three desk types, to suit the different companies working in the building. "Fixed desks," located in the open-plan area of the floor, are hired by a business for their own sole use and are adjacent to other fixed desks. This means the different creative businesses can interact with each other and create an energetic working environment, where serendipitous exchange of ideas can take place. "Open office desks" are also located in the open-plan area, but

at its perimeter, offering more privacy. "Closed office desks" are located within partitioned spaces at the perimeter of the plan, giving full privacy to the occupants.

○ **Decoration**

Bespoke desks were designed to feel more like a shared table than a piece of office furniture, though individuals still have their own defined space to work in. A series of oversized rugs in the workspaces feature bespoke patterns based on original motifs found within the building, created by Squire and Partners and south London design duo Eley Kishimoto, who took inspiration from the music, energy, and heritage of the client, multimedia entertainment business Ministry of Sound.

○ **Design elements**

Designers took the bold, raw elements of the former Victorian printworks and contrasted them with a layer of premium finish to create

a "premium raw" aesthetic. This was used to establish a creative and energetic environment that transforms throughout the day and into the evening, shifting tempo as the working week progresses, and staying true to the origins of the mother brand.

The innovative origins of Ministry of Sound and the raw factory space have been fused with refined elements including furniture, fabrics, lighting, and artworks. Original exposed timber floors, untreated textured walls and black painted steelwork provide a canvas for a carefully curated layer that defines a series of relaxed hospitality spaces.

Circulation spaces between the floors reveal original terrazzo stairs in hues of pale green and pink, and exposed concrete and steel structure.

The petrol blue of the building's original lift doors inspired the color palette of the furniture, and the use of black throughout the design ties in with the branding of The Ministry. The conscious omission of a traditional logo-heavy identity for the workspace affords the creative community the freedom to have breathing room for their own businesses, without feeling subservient to the history or heritage of an imposed brand.

The design goes against the grain of traditional workspace interiors, with an approach that blurs the lines between work and play. This aesthetic is carried through to all senses, using a carefully crafted layer of visual stimulus, house scents, curated soundscapes for interior and exterior spaces (devised by a sound architect to form a variety of audio sensory environments) along with guest services to create a holistic experience for residents and visitors.

The Shop at the Contemporary Arts Center

Location / New Orleans, Louisiana

Completion / 2017

Area / 40,000 square feet (3,716 square meters)

Client / The Domain Companies

Design / EskewDumezRipple

Photography / Neil Alexander, Sara Essex Bradley

EskewDumezRipple is a New Orleans–based architecture, interiors, and urban-planning firm recognized for producing innovative projects grounded by a strong understanding of context, culture, and environment.

Established in 1989, EskewDumezRipple has transformed from a local firm doing nationally recognized work to a national firm that has retained its local roots. Recipient of the prestigious Architecture Firm Award from the American Institute of Architects in 2014, the firm has continued to find meaningful ways to shape community and the profession at large. Building upon the legacy of its founder Allen Eskew, the firm strives to engage the world as he did—with humility, charm, and a deeply personal commitment to design as craft.

○ **The space**

Envisioned as the cornerstone of what is quickly becoming the region's "innovation corridor," The Shop sits at the nexus of many of the city's most important cultural institutions. The project occupies the third and fourth floors of the New Orleans Contemporary Arts Center (CAC). Working within the context of the historic building, the design team slowly peeled away layers of interior floors and walls to make a lively two-story atrium that exudes warmth and texture. Visitors enter the building first via this atrium, and then ascend upwards to the third and fourth floors via an exposed mesh-clad elevator. Upon passing reception, visitors enter into the heart of the space, The Commons, designed to facilitate communication and conversation among members. It boasts a full kitchen, beer and coffee taps, and communal and recreation space.

Exposing and enhancing the existing conditions was a unifying aspect throughout design. Special care was made in opening the interior to the structural foundation, creating a tectonic contrast of modern interior design and rustic, heavy timber framing. Inspiration was also taken from the idea of intertwining art and handmade elements, with the feature stair that connects the two floors serving as a distinct example of this ethos. Similarly, from a programming standpoint, functional areas were designed to support the interweaving of people from diverse backgrounds. The idea was to create a space where members of various organizations and occupations could cross paths and spark chance conversations, affording opportunities for networking and collaboration.

The third floor comprises reception, and main lounge area and event space, café, private office, hot desks, conference rooms, private phone booths, meeting booths and restrooms. The fourth floor also has hot desks, private phone booths, meeting booths, and restrooms, as well as a large conference room, coffee bar, the owner's office, and private offices.

In addition to the anchor tenant spaces, there is a variety of office sizes meant to accommodate individuals or companies comprising up to 10 employees. The Commons on the third floor was designed with a generous amount of space for public events, screenings, and workshops.

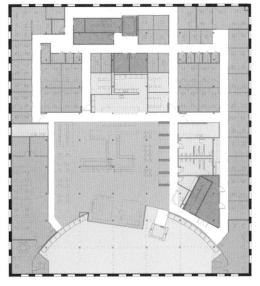

Third-floor plan

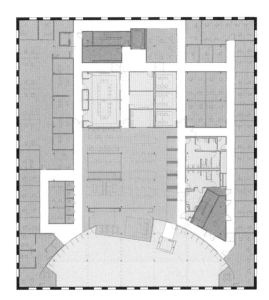

Fourth-floor plan

▨ Private offices
▨ The Commons
▨ Conference rooms / shared amenities
▨ Back of house / mechanical rooms

The café and kitchen area, similarly affording a generous amount of space, serve as an extension of this area. Standard conference rooms can seat six people, with a large conference room designed to seat 20.

○ **The flow**

Double-loaded corridors access offices and conference rooms, all of which extend to The Commons. Radiating out from this central area are private offices, clustered on the perimeter for privacy and access to daylight. This intervention made it possible for The Commons to serve as a community asset, accessible to everyone.

Expanding upon this notion, all shared functions and amenities are in this central area, including the copy room, conference rooms, restrooms, and café. To this end, nearly everyone entering The Shop

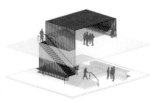

Axonometric

passes through this common area. This creates the sense of an overall open plan, while still allowing privacy. With all central amenities centrally located, the circulation and flow easily alleviate wayfinding concerns.

○ **Dividing the space**

Transparency was paramount in the project's design. Private offices were enclosed with glass to maximize daylight coming into The Commons and to showcase the existing structure—a mix of

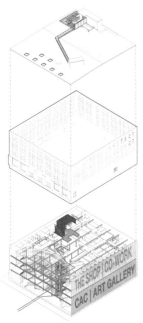

Axonometric

historic masonry and heavy timber. Feature stairs and furniture were also used to define the space of The Commons—the platform of the feature stair was used to create unconventional pockets for informal gatherings and unorthodox working styles. Booths were used to screen the restrooms and provide alternative work experiences—this has the added benefit of making them private but feel connected.

○ **Decoration**

A custom-designed reception desk of wood and black metal slats takes cues from the stair. Entryway lighting is meant to create a playful ambiance. Throughout, the design features comfortable lounge furniture sourced from a variety of vendors and vintage pieces to bring a sense of the living room to an office setting. Hot desks and fixed banquettes accommodate different types of work and the lighting was organized to delineate a wide variety of seating experiences and to accent key features like custom murals that were commissioned throughout the space. Local and national artists were brought in to adorn the walls, connecting the co-working tenants with the art community.

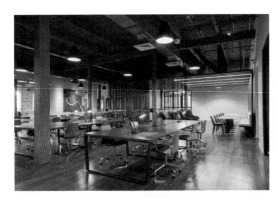

(Before)

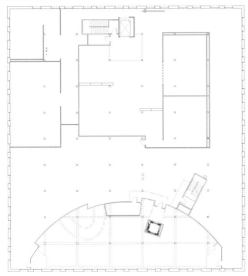

(After)

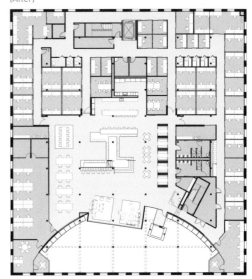

Third-floor plan

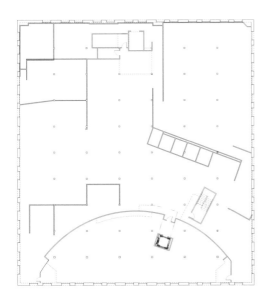

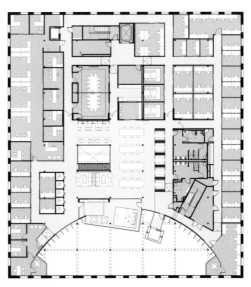

Fourth-floor plan

○ **Design elements**

Mural walls were part of the design. The space could then host local artists to come in to create additional artworks. The space has also been curated with pieces from local artists, extending the theme of drawing inspiration from the CAC itself, and the space's symbolic place in the community as an enclave for artistic expression. The conference rooms each had a theme that was drawn from artistic disciplines (theater, dance, visual and performing arts), creating opportunities to vary wall coverings and furniture within, as well as lighting fixtures.

AGP eGlass Factory & Offices

Location / Lima, Peru

Completion / 2015

Area / 107,639 square feet (10,000 square meters)

Client / AGP eGlass

Design / V.Oid/Felipe Ferrer

Photography / Juan Solano, Nicolas Villaume

V.Oid is an architecture and design studio that works in a range of projects—it takes anything that is interesting and has the potential to question, play, and change the status quo. Its trans-disciplinary approach fluctuates between art, architecture, advertisement, and design. In 2015 V.Oid was nominated for the Mies Crown Hall Americas Prize (MCHAP) for its AGP eGlass project, a factory and office facility that produces windshields for Tesla cars, including the Model X—the largest windscreen ever produced for a passenger car. The project was also awarded a Golden A'Design Award in 2015, and a silver award at the AAP American Architecture Prize in 2016.

◯ The space

As AGP produces glass for car windshields, cleanness is crucial. Going through an entry corridor wrapped in black carpet, the ceiling height shrinks to have a buffer space between the street and the lobby, then the funnel-shaped space opens up toward a vertical triple-height cylindrical space that is wrapped in 19 feet (6 meters) of LED-backlit U glass. The white walls, floor, and ceiling polarize the dark entry funnel. The reception desk is made of raw glass that has been built like a flat brick wall. The cylinder is disrupted by a cantilevered glass prism that hovers over the entry; this space is the boardroom, and after walking up the glass stairs this is the first space you encounter. The boardroom is enclosed with switchable glass and is not typically used in privacy mode, in line with the idea that the offices should always have a visual

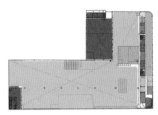

Second-floor function space

First-floor function space

Office space
Director office
Showroom
Electric substation
Boardroom
Industrial space

connection to the production line. The showroom is enclosed by three black glass walls and atmospheric music is activated when someone walks in.

The office area works as a big space with open meeting rooms. An inner glass façade reinforces the visual connection between offices and industry line. All the first floor has a light blue tinted glass and all the glass above is white and ultra-clear glass. The black, low-lit stairs act like a palate cleanser, while the yellow handrail hints at a highway line; the lighting is located underneath.

On the second floor above the lobby, a white-lit corridor with epoxy white floor frames the entrance to meeting rooms, laboratories, testing rooms, and research and development (R&D) spaces. The dining area acts as a hub for the offices, laboratories, and changing rooms for operators and engineers, connecting the back entrance of the facilities.

The production offices hover over the production line with a clear view of most of the areas; attached to this structure, a glass floor bridge cantilevers from the corner as a lookout spot.

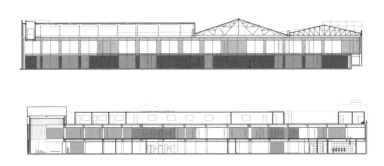

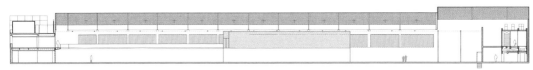

Section plans

○ **The flow**

The project has two entrances: the main entrance is for workers in the administrative offices and the second is for the industrial-space workers. To get to the office space, workers need to pass through security clearance and the facilities hall. This space delivers to the laboratory, R&D on the first floor and to the second floor for the administrative offices. On the first floor, the spaces are connected by a corridor on the right side of the facility next to the façade; this is below street level, so the laboratory and R&D are located next to the industrial space for easy access and better illumination. At the end of the corridor, the dining room, kitchen, and facilities are connected to the secondary access for workers. These connections have access restrictions because of the confidentiality of the spaces.

On the second floor, a corridor connects through the center of the space; on the left is the boardroom, directors' offices, managers' offices, kitchenettes, and meeting rooms, while on the right is the open office space. At the end of the corridor, rooms are located next to the industrial space, which is enclosed by glass walls that permit transparency from

any part of the open-space offices. These offices are on the right next to the façade to take advantage of natural lighting. The industrial space can be accessed by the hall or the secondary access, and has a proper pedestrian path for an industrial line, which leads to auxiliary spaces. A warehouse area at the back of the facilities provides storage of final products and materials, and is accessible via the industrial space or another entrance.

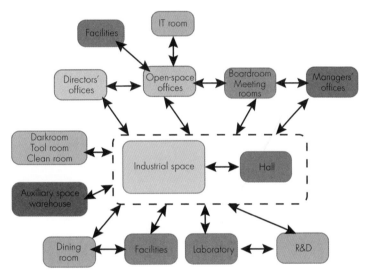

The flow

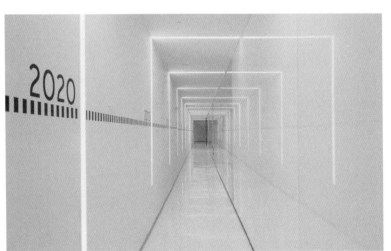

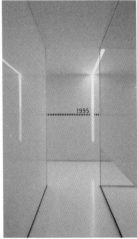

○ Dividing the space

The project is divided into two main functional spaces—an industrial space and an administrative office area, divided by a curtain wall to give them a direct visual connection. On the second floor the office area has an overpass that cantilevers to the industrial space, designed for clients who might need a visit to the industrial space without going into it. The overpass has glass guardrails, in order to keep the transparency and the visual connection from the office area, and connects directly to a

(Before)

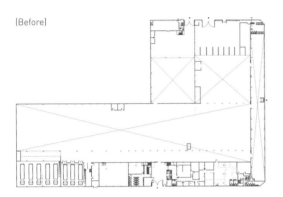

(After)

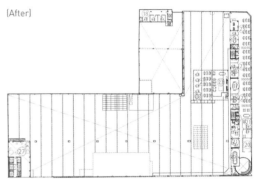

Second-floor plan

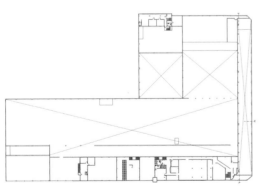

First-floor plan

① Hall
② Laboratory
③ R&D
④ Dining room
⑤ Kitchen
⑥ Vertical circulation
⑦ Facilities / changing
⑧ Serigraphy room
⑨ Tool room
⑩ Darkroom
⑪ Tool room 2
⑫ Facilities
⑬ Pre-clean room
⑭ Clean room
⑮ Warehouse
⑯ Industrial space
⑰ Meeting room
⑱ Auxiliary office space
⑲ Boardroom
⑳ Showroom
㉑ Directors' offices
㉒ Toilets
㉓ Office space
㉔ Kitchenette
㉕ Managers' offices
㉖ IT room
㉗ Electric substation

production office over the industrial line. Divided by glass, it resembles a fish tank with 360-degree views over the industrial space.

All the dividers and partitions are built-in glass. On the first floor, transparent and opaque blue glass was used for confidential areas, while on the second floor designers used ultra-clear glass and opaque white glass to cover vertical circulation and columns. In the interior of the office area, partitions between offices were built in opaque white glass, and between the open space and managers' offices the ultra-clear glass contains gradient films to maintain some privacy but keep

visual connections with the whole project. For spaces like the darkroom, IT room, and showroom, that needed more intimacy, black opaque glass was used.

○ **Decoration**

Despite the technological image expressed by the use of glass and white clean spaces, accents of colors and materials were used in the office area to create a warm environment to work in. The managers' offices, kitchenettes, and meeting rooms were coded with lemon-colored glass and oak wood. Ceilings and carpets were used to optimize the acoustics in offices and meeting rooms. Meeting tables are in oak wood, with white and gray chairs. In the open-space areas, small tables are also made from oak but desks are white.

The industrial space contains white epoxy floor, and blackout tensile textile for walls and ceiling. The lighting and ventilation are joined together in one slot on the ceiling to minimize the visual noise. The dry, non-chemical nature of the production line allowed the use of materials that traditionally would not be used in an industrial space. The south façade has a double-insulated U glass channel to bring light but protect from the heat of the summer sun exposure. The rest of the façade is clad in silver aluminum panels, while the base of the volume is painted dark gray and takes advantage of the sloped sidewalk to emphasize the main entrance without a bigger gesture.

○ Design elements

The project adapted to an existing storage facility, with the objective of saving as much as possible of the existing steel roof structure with its exterior cover. The office space originally was a double-height concrete-and-brick storage area.

The client wanted state-of-the-art installations to build trust with their clients, mostly auto makers from the United States and Europe. The brief of the project was for a space that would inspire the people that work there, and encourage the operators and engineers to work as clean as possible, and to create a stimulating office space that maximized transparency and visibility toward the industrial line.

Detsky Mir Headquarters

Location / Moscow, Russia

Completion / 2018

Area / 59,201 square feet (5,500 square meters)

Client / Detsky Mir

Design / FORM bureau

Photography / Ilya Ivanov

FORM bureau is a multi-disciplinary practice founded in Moscow in 2011 by architects Vera Odyn and Olga Treivas. FORM has completed over 80 projects in Europe and Latin America. The bureau's main area of interest is in museums and educational institutions, developing both architecture and internal scenarios, such as exhibitions, libraries, and cafés.

○ The space

The office is the headquarters of children's retailer Detsky Mir, and so the board game proved to be a fruitful analogy for conceiving the office layout. Its constituents of field, grid, and playing figure characterize the various typologies of space.

The reception zone marks the starting point of the game, with cues that gather the entire idea of the office in one place. Recognizable symbols of Detsky Mir, such as its logo colors, shop windows, and toys, become functional objects that greet the visitor. Next is the playing field of open-plan workspace, with navigation signs becoming a pattern on the floor used to direct flow.

○ Dividing the space

The space is divided into several principal zones. There is a reception area that is mirrored on other floors as a lounge zone that greets visitors

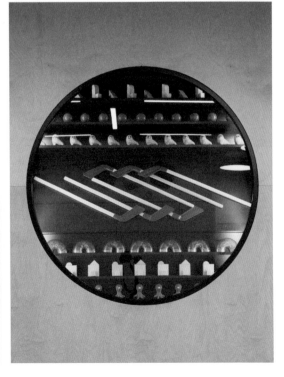

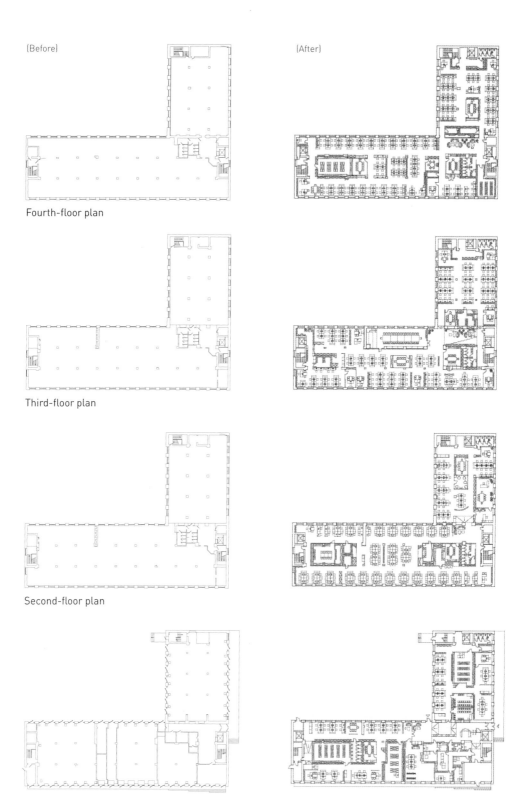

(Before)

(After)

Fourth-floor plan

Third-floor plan

Second-floor plan

First-floor plan

in front of the lifts. Next one enters an open-plan work environment with work tables taking up space along the windows, while the central darker areas are used for circulation and facilities that require closed rooms. The central volumes were considered as markers or game figures, which function as focal points within a neutral interior and house meeting rooms, staff dining areas, and storage facilities. These zones are placed in the playing field of the office as game blocks appearing on the route. They also function as a spatial divider between the various departments. Their design is based on an abstraction of well-known games such as backgammon and pinball.

○ **The dimensions**

The spatial division was dictated by the brief as well as limitations of the existing building, a printing factory built during the 1970s. The task was to house various departments of Detsky Mir, taking into account particular seating requirements, neighboring departments, a set number of meeting rooms and storage as well as room for expansion. The total floor area is 59,201 square feet (5,500 square meters). The four open-plan floors offer over 600 workspaces.

In order to meet requirements, the central space on each floor had to be doubled up. It forms a condensed core where the lower areas often house storage and service rooms, while a second level is opened up and used as meeting space.

○ **Decoration**

Most of the items for the project were designed and made to order. Meeting rooms, wardrobes and storage areas, partitions, lighting systems and lamps, and upholstered furniture were designed by FORM bureau. Simple bold forms and allusions to childhood games and toys can be traced in the geometry of the objects.

Color coding played an important role in the project. The four brand colors of Detsky Mir meet in the reception area, and are then spread across the four floors in the form of a grid lighting structure. Each of the four floors is assigned a color—blue, green, yellow, or red. One strong primary color is supported by more subtle pastel shades on each floor.

The idea of board games is carried through into meeting-room designs. Popular games such as backgammon, noughts and crosses, and pinball were distilled into bold recognizable patterns that define and name each meeting room.

Certain repeating elements such as partitions in the form of giant grass and soft furnishings play with the idea of distorted proportion related to childhood imagination.

Ornamental pattern displays were created in the reception area to echo toy-shop windows. Another important element is a small museum of Soviet toys at the entrance to the workspace on the first floor.

○ Design elements

Two central ideas characterize the project: distorted proportion and the workplace as a board game. Distorted proportion is about the sense of largeness and altered perception that children experience, where objects and spaces are seen not for their rational functional value, but as playscapes onto which the imagination projects an expanded reality. This was used in the approach to form, furnishings, and decorative elements across the office. Across the floor there are illustrations positioned at key focal points. These were largely influenced by murals and artistic signage that would signify various types of produce within the original Detsky Mir department store. Wherever possible the designers aimed to create a visual connection between the different work areas.

Goodman Offices

Location / Madrid, Spain

Completion / 2017

Area / 1,604 square feet (149 square meters)

Client / Goodman Offices

Design / Zooco Estudio

Photography / Imagen Subliminal

Zooco Estudio is a young architectural firm founded in 2008 by Miguel Crespo Picot, Javier Guzmán Benito, and Sixto Martín Martínez, with head offices in Madrid and Santander. Its philosophy is to face each project, from interior interventions to building large structures, through the same creative process. Developing projects with different scales, architectural decisions are always the same: to create spaces that respond to needs and environment, always based on the generation of a clear concept as the base of the project. This vision of architecture, and the flexibility to adapt to different projects, has made the firm understand its profession at a time of social and economic change.

○ **The space**

With the establishment of the Goodman Offices project, the firm found an open space, where the nucleus of the toilets, the structure, and the glass façade were the only aspects to take into account. A linear circulation was created around the whole space.

○ **The flow**

The space division is achieved by two wooden partitions strung with strings in a lattice pattern. It follows the space, creating areas such as reception, meeting rooms, and reprography room, and it also turns into furniture, as it can be used for lockers, storage, and kitchen space, allowing more or less vision depending on client needs.

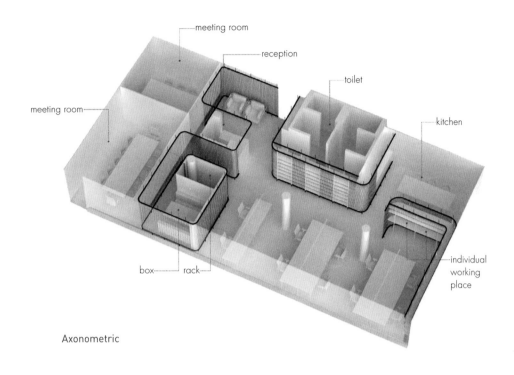

meeting room
reception
toilet
kitchen
meeting room
box rack
individual working place

Axonometric

(Before)

(After)

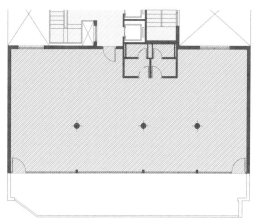
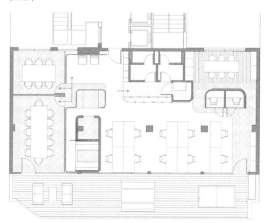

Floor plan

The office contains few fixed places, but instead provides various ways of having a meeting and working together, with a lot of flexibility for different situations.

○ **Decoration**

Green and gray colors were used for carpets and fittings. Custom-designed fittings include glass partitions in an extruded aluminum setting, as well as the central wooden partitions using a lattice of green and gray elastic polypropylene strings. Chairs, desks, and tables were sourced from a variety of designers.

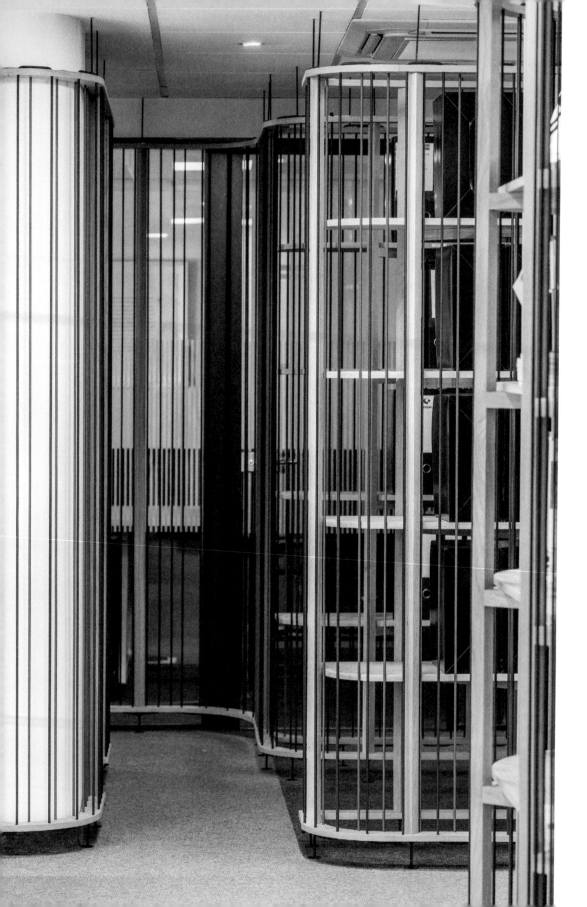

Lighting was designed to come from a wide range of sources, including recessed rail lights and spotlights, as well as suspended and pendant lamps.

○ Design elements

The main request from the owners was to create a space for their way of doing business: it is about an office in which there are few fixed places, but instead various ways of having a meeting and working together, with a lot of flexibility.

The answer to these requirements was to produce a unique language that goes through the office, creating space for the different uses and circulations required. For that purpose, designers used the wooden partitions made with elastic strings as a generator of the project. The areas relate to each other through the main element, which creates the spaces and caters to every need and function.

Guateque Office

Location / Mexico City, Mexico
Completion / 2016
Area / 7,771 square feet (722 square meters)

Client / Guateque
Design / Estudio Atemporal
Photography / LGM Studio

Estudio Atemporal is a studio founded in Mexico City in 2011 by Paul Curuchet and Luciana de la Garza. Architects work closely with a multidisciplinary team, from the conception of the project to its materialization, and covering all aspects from architecture and furniture to visual identity. From the beginning, they have had an interest in diversifying their work as much as possible, exploring different architectural typologies. They have worked on around 50 projects, most of which they also built. Consideration of the history of a space to understand the present and endure in the future is an indispensable methodology in Estudio Atemporal's design process.

○ The space

The space consists of two large areas: a warehouse with a structure based on columns and a saw-tooth roof, and a three-level building.

When the project began there were two different accesses, as the former industrial space contained two independent buildings over a whole block that were part of the same complex but not connected to each other. When the client decided to rent the two buildings, they wanted to have just one main entrance with an access control and a reception. A door was created to have a new connection, integrating these two areas into one.

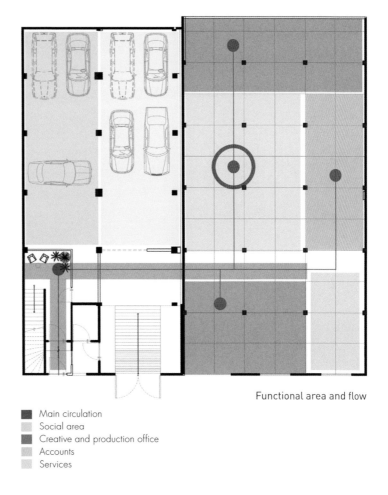

Functional area and flow

- ▀ Main circulation
- ▀ Social area
- ▀ Creative and production office
- ▀ Accounts
- ▀ Services

Each area has a clear relationship with each other, understanding that every department of this office works independently but they need each other in order to complete the work to the final stage.

○ The flow

The new front door became the starting point, leading to the main area, what became known as "the workshop," where a central area becomes the connection point between the other spaces and a perfect place for recreation and other activities. In this area it is possible to see everyone working; everyone in the building is connected to this place, and metaphorically it represents the collaboration between each person.

(Before)

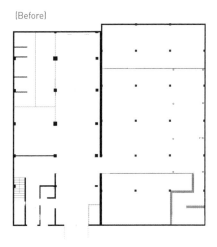

(After)

First-floor plan

Mezzanine plan

○ **Dividing the space**

In dividing the space, consideration was given to areas being private and still being connected to the outside; having the option of closing doors to reduce the noise or opening them to take down the barriers.

On one side of the workshop space there is a production office and on the other is the creative office. Their way of working is very different but in the end they need to collaborate a lot to make things happen. Considering this, the design was really important to the offices working together well. A big structure with transparent glass divided the areas and connected them at the same time; even if the doors are closed you can feel the space as a coherent whole. A smaller area for client accounts is placed by the mezzanine.

○ Decoration and design elements

Exposed cinder-block walls and concrete columns were retained. All the furniture was designed specifically for this office after an analysis of what was needed for each area. The space was designed to be clean and neutral, in line with the structure of the building, so contrast was brought in with the furniture, adding some colors carefully selected to harmonize with the rest of the elements. Primary and secondary colors were mostly used.

Skanska Headquarters

Location / Budapest, Hungary

Completion / 2017

Area / 5,1667 square feet (480 square meters)

Client / Skanska

Design / LAB5 architects

Photography / Zsolt Batár

LAB5 architects is a design studio working on both sides of the wall; the team of architects and interior designers uses creative solutions for a diverse palette of residential, office, and public buildings. Scale is from the tiniest objects of the interior to large-scale buildings.

The studio was founded by four partners 10 years ago in Budapest, Hungary, and works globally from Asia to America, always providing a unique design, focusing on the flow of the people using the city and the buildings, and creating green solutions.

○ The space

When designing an interior, a strong vision or great idea has to be balanced against how best to use the space that is already there. Ideally they can work together and strengthen each other when linked with an understanding of the needs of the owner and future users.

In this case, designers had to create an office interior in a traditional office building. The client, Swedish development and construction group Skanska, gave them details about how they expected the office to be used—how many people would use the office at once, what they did at their desks, how they ate, how meetings were held—as well as a "wish list" that included a lounge area for relaxation. The designers could visualize how big tables and other surfaces needed to be, how many meters of shelves they need for storage and so on.

Most importantly they wanted a super-flexible office layout, so all their workstations were placed in the same space. Staff wanted to keep their kitchenette hidden in the background only for themselves, but also wanted their visitors to feel comfortable when they saw a kitchen counter and glass fridge close to the entrance. So designers separated some of the regular kitchen functions, with some parts standing exposed at the entrance, while other parts were left in the back area. Lounge corners were needed in the open space, and were also requested for relaxation, so two separate lounge areas were designed. A big company meeting is held every week, so designers designed them a little amphitheater that staff can use as a flexible area on most days, and it can be used as a big meeting area once a week.

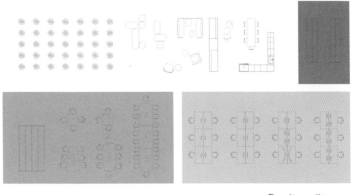

Furniture diagram

○ The flow

On analysis of the site, three questions emerged as the most important questions. How can they place all the workstations close—less than 16 feet (5 meters)—to the windows to provide enough natural light? How can they provide a transition between the public area where clients arrive, sit, and have meetings, and the space where only the employees of the company can go? How can they provide the big area for the weekly company meeting?

Designers started to place the public functions such as meeting rooms, open kitchenette, and receptionist, close to the entrance. They placed all the workstations at the windows. And they put the storage areas, the server room, the archive, and the closed kitchenette in the back of the space behind a shaft. They ended up having all functions at their best possible location, and gained an open area in the middle, like a field in the middle of a forest, where it can be used flexibly.

People arriving are directed to the receptionists and to the guest kitchen counter, where they can sit down, ask if they need information, wait for the meeting to start, and go to the meeting rooms. By placing the field with the amphitheater in the middle they created a flow around it, which integrates all the corridors of the open space.

○ Dividing the space

Designers were sure that this company values transparency, as well as the sharing of space. They wanted to show this to arriving guests, while at the same time avoiding all arrivals being able to see every workstation, so they needed an element right in front of the entrance door. The came up with a "forest," a positive element that also creates a nice atmosphere and is a reminder of the character of the company. It is a reminder of the natural feel of the Swedish firm, and a strong positive atmospheric element as well as a tool for space division.

In the case of meeting rooms designers had to envelope some rooms because of acoustic expectations, but they opened up those boxes by using glazed walls as much as possible, allowing natural light to travel across the entire space, and as a reminder of the core value of transparency.

The amphitheater in the middle divides the rest of the open space into areas as it is needed, and the slope of the seated surface hides the copy machines in the back, while those can be still placed in the same open office space. Designers used walls to cover the back functions and covered them with the lockers where the employees can hold their personal belongings.

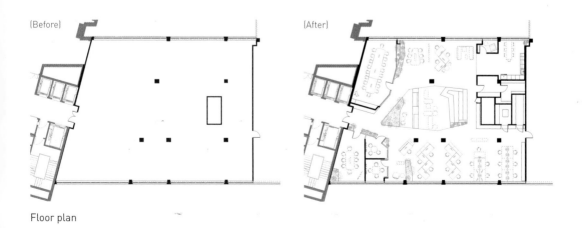

(Before)　　　　　　　　　　　(After)

Floor plan

○ **Decoration and design elements**

After designers found the keywords and created the strongest interior-design element in the middle of the space, they subordinated all design detail to this vision of the strong feeling of nature. They placed the "forest" in other parts of the office where privacy was needed, and picked the white and light-blue colors for all painted elements to create a feeling of being outdoors under the sky. Wood was used where they had to build bigger pieces of furniture. They removed the suspended ceiling where possible to gain more height, and to expose the rustic surface of the slab above it.

All the elements have created one strong visual effect; like a river, the flow of the space provides details to look at, or different atmospheres for working in. The idea was to feel natural, so designers followed the concept: there are some clouds hanging under the ceiling, there is a bird's nest in the bushes, and there are little rocks where the ground was too steep.

dosa by DOSA

Location / Oakland, United States

Completion / 2017

Area / 3,530 square feet (328 square meters)

Client / dosa by DOSA

Design / Feldman Architecture

Photography / Kassie Borreson

Feldman Architecture is an innovative residential and commercial design practice recognized for creating warm, light-filled spaces that are site-sensitive and carefully detailed. Highly collaborative in nature, the firm approaches design as a dialogue between client, design team, and site. Each project is an opportunity to create an innovative solution that is relevant to the project environs and tailored to a client's specific needs.

○ **The space**

The clients for restaurant dosa by DOSA went through a soul-searching design process that resulted in a program that would work all day, from breakfast through dinner with a high capacity for happy hour. It is a fast casual concept, intended to scale to multiple locations. The objective was to create an authentic space for Indian cuisine that would help the public better understand the rich food and culture from the streets of Mumbai while maintaining the characteristics of the uptown Oakland neighborhood and honoring the sophistication of the clients.

The space was a challenge, being shoehorned between two commercial office spaces above and below. Extra measures had to be taken to eliminate sound transfer through the ceilings and the walls while maintaining a crisp aesthetic, and exhaust had to be routed out from under a mezzanine space occupied by the other tenant to the roof above. The opportunity was taken to create a large vertical element that anchored the space and allowed for the mechanical ductwork to be hidden, leaving only the original wood truss ceiling exposed.

(Before)

Floor plan

(After)

① Entry / outdoor seating
② Communal dining table
③ Dining
④ Bar
⑤ Kitchen

○ **The flow**

The restaurant space has a central catwalk leading the customer from the entry to the ordering counter and then to the dosa window. The catwalk is designated by a decorative tile pattern that fades out toward the dining and bar areas. The floor pattern mimics the circulation of the space, with the most complex patterning in the high-traffic zones, then dissipating out to the calmer zones, weathering as though the circulation has revealed the history worn below.

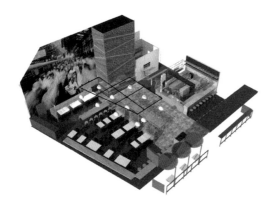

Axonometric

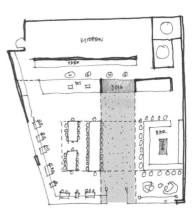

Sketch

○ **Dividing the space**

The experience at dosa by DOSA is guided by its architectural simplicity. Upon entering the space, the "unconventional bar" to the right acts as the primary point of contact for customer and wait staff before maneuvering guests into the crosswise dining area. The architecture greets you. The focus was to make the space intuitive and give customers control over their own participation. Without a traditional hostess and wait staff, visitors are encouraged to navigate their own journey through the restaurant, instructed by its straightforward symmetry and design.

○ The dimensions

The double-height space is wrapped by the mezzanine of a neighboring tenant. The designers wanted the dining area to be located under the historic wood-framed vaulted ceiling while still facing out toward the street. The kitchen was designed to be tucked away in the back of house in the single-height space, but also centrally located to allow visibility of the handcrafted food. The bar was thoughtfully tucked into the neighboring single-height area. The mechanical systems that bring fresh air in and push the hot air out needed to be shrouded in the central space. The designers used this opportunity to create a wooden hearth to conceal the extensive ductwork moving from the kitchen and out through the roof. This feature guides the eye from the compressed bar area out and up into the double-height space, celebrating the existing wood and brick construction.

○ Decoration

Designers used the words "energetic," "edgy," and "easygoing" to create an all-day bar, large communal gathering area, and intimate seating

options while preserving the historic character of the brick-and-timber building. The detailed patterns and textures are modern interpretations of traditional patterns employed in tile, wood, marble, and brass. Two large-scale murals, one depicting an iconic street scene and the other an inspired ode to Oakland, were done in collaboration with local Oakland artists. The goal was to root an authentic Indian street vibe in the center of Oakland. The large vertical wooded shroud creates an energetic yet warm hearth, opening views to the handcrafted dosas being flipped on the griddle beyond.

○ **Design elements**

At dosa by DOSA, the eye is constantly pulled through the complex but subtle palette that highlights the craft of the space and its enlivened cultural center.

The restaurant uses five distinct patterns to create a comprehensive vibe that is simultaneously cohesive and unique. The wood pattern of the shroud, the geometric pattern of the screens, the hexagonal pattern of the floor tile, the printed pattern on the floor tile, and the marble veining all work in tandem to add character to the space. All of these unique features are authentic plays on traditional Indian patterns.

The restaurant also employs five attractor points; the dosa window, the ordering counter, the bar, the street mural, and, during special events, the drop-down projection screen. These, in combination with the street scene, create a lively backdrop from every perspective.

Eberly

Location / Austin, United States
Completion / 2016
Area / 15,000 square feet (1,394 square meters)

Client / John Scott, Eddy Patterson, Michael Dickson, Mickie Spencer
Design / Clayton & Little (architecture), Mickie Spencer (interior design)
Photography / Merrick Ales, Chloe Hope Gilstrap

Clayton & Little is an interdisciplinary design firm known for creating layered, coherent experiences by filtering context and intent to summon the richness of place.

Emily Little founded her Austin firm in 1983 with a commitment to making good design accessible and attainable, and an interest in the adaptive reuse of historic structures. Paul Clayton joined Emily's firm in 2001 and together, they evolved the practice. In 2005, Paul acquired Emily's firm and continues to lead it today with partners, directors, and design leads across a range of disciplines.

In 2015, the firm expanded from Austin to San Antonio after completing several high-profile projects in Alamo City. The second office joins more than 30 architects and designers with a long history of working together in the two cities while broadening the firm's range of services to incorporate architecture, interior design, experience design, brand, and identity. The beneficial exchange of ideas across the region has impacted locations outside of Texas; recent expansion includes projects in California, Hawaii, Maryland, and beyond.

○ The space

Painting a thorough picture of the spatial sequences at Eberly reveals Clayton & Little's approach to all projects, whether commercial or residential: creating spaces that evoke the richness of each unique place. At Eberly, varied spaces and quirky yet elegant interiors come together to elicit the soul of Austin.

Intended to reflect the Texas capital city's independent spirit, Eberly was conceived to be a gathering place where risk-takers, creative types, and liberated thinkers could connect and feed off each other's energy and creativity. The establishment's visually layered spaces support this intent.

As patrons enter the Eberly Dining Room, a darker, almost brooding atmosphere weighs on the space. The moody darkness is punctured by

the light-filled Study immediately adjacent to the entry which draws the eye to and through the space back to the historic Cedar Tavern.

Opposite the Study, a beaming brass-clad kitchen commands the space at the heart of the restaurant. Beyond the pulsing kitchen, guests are met yet again by a darker space that anchors the back of the building, the Cedar Tavern. Here, friends and contemporaries gather, drink, think, and dine late into the night.

At Clayton & Little, working through spatial sequences allows the firm to get to the heart of the problem through a deep analysis of what a space does and does not want to be. In this case, given the size of the original building, the newly configured space had to be broken into smaller spaces to bring it down to human scale. They could have ended up as separate rooms, though a segmented solution would not have spoken to the tapestry of cultures, thoughts, and experiences that make Austin such a beloved city.

Further contributing to the layers, the rich interiors deftly mix and match styles from the mid-mod Eberly Dining Room to the industrial Study to the refined yet gritty Cedar Tavern.

Section

○ The flow

Creating a spatial flow to result in a memorable experience necessitated carving up the 10,000-square-foot (929-square-meter) footprint. Skillful visual layering and spatial connectivity along with stylistically distinct yet complementary interiors serve as an invitation for patrons to explore the restaurant. A few notes to highlight:

A central, light-filled space serves as a visual spine to connect the entire length of the restaurant from the Eberly Dining Room back to the Cedar Tavern.

A wide circulation path invites diners to see the action in the kitchen, teasing their palates while piquing their interest in the process and creating a buzz.

The ground-level Private Bar and Cannon Room, only accessible from a nondescript service door on the exterior, are hidden from sight directly behind the Cedar Tavern. This arrangement creates a speakeasy vibe well suited for private events with a direct connection to the kitchen.

The rooftop patio and bar, accessed from the outside adjacent to the Cedar Tavern, are reserved for private events.

The round banquettes in the Eberly Dining Room along with the large, low lounge seating in the Cedar Tavern foster communal conversation.

The outdoor patio shares a glass wall with the Study, creating a clear visual connection through all spaces terminating at the kitchen.

○ **Dividing the space**

The spatial division was largely driven by the existing column grid and the existing concrete masonry unit wall layout. The dividing wall between

the Eberly Dining Room and Study shared the line that separated the original print shop front offices from the rear floor production. Designers worked within the existing structural modules to create balanced, proportionate spaces to satisfy their constraints.

Circulation and flow dictated the secondary organizing principle. The Study and Kitchen hallway serve as the central spine connecting the Eberly Dining Room back to the Cedar Tavern. The Kitchen mirrors this central spine containing its own back of house circulation spine to organize the kitchen and storage functions.

Finally, design iterations were worked back and forth between seating layouts, bar configurations, and kitchen layouts to create comfortable spaces that promote visual connections, and invite exploration and discovery of spaces.

Designers were given an interesting, fairly open building to work with from the beginning. They kept the existing ceiling heights wherever possible in order to showcase the concrete panels, but recognized that at certain locations they needed to compress spaces to bring them to human scale.

To deliver on the owner's intent of a more intimate space, the Eberly Dining Room features a lowered, coffered ceiling to set the tone upon entry. To significantly open the Study with light and make it airy, designers opened the roof above it, extended a skylight monitor through the roof, and increased the ceiling height. The interplay between the Dining Room and Study is key to changing the mood between spaces. This produces varied dining experiences, and options that work together to create an overall rich experience.

① Entry
② Main dining
③ Main bar
④ Study
⑤ Outdoor patio
⑥ Cedar Tavern
⑦ Cannon Room
⑧ Washroom
⑨ Kitchen
⑩ Kitchen storage

(Before)

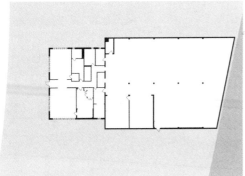

(After)

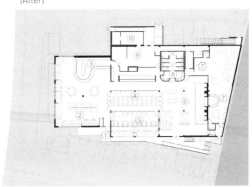

First-floor plan

○ Decoration

Speaking to the rich history of the Cedar Tavern, brown and oxblood tufted leather sofas surround coffee tables in a lounge configuration to promote gathering and conversations. Vibrant blue barstools with brass tacks contrast with the mahogany bar, while gold and purple ottomans are arranged throughout to enliven darker, rich tones. Brass serves to unify all spaces, and is showcased in custom designed and fabricated light fixtures that surround the columns.

The Study takes cues from the Cedar Tavern, but features more simplified furniture so as not to detract from the light-filled steel structure. Carefully curated books, curios, and plants adorn the walls, creating a sense of a lived-in space. Custom designed and fabricated wall sconces continue the industrial character of the steel and utilize heat-sink fins to create the unique style of the lights.

Pulling in wood from the Cedar Tavern, walnut is the main focus in the Eberly Dining Room, and helps deliver its desired moody atmosphere. Vibrancy is toned down with selectively used velvet upholstery featured only at central and perimeter banquette seating. A large central banquette accommodates larger groups while remaining flexible enough to separate out for smaller parties. Ample banquette seating was chosen to foster the notion of the place as ideal for gathering, thinking, drinking, and dining.

○ **Design elements**

Careful attention was given to the look and feel of each individual space. The interior design reinforces the spatial organization and adds masterfully to its visual layering. Dark woods, velvet banquettes, brass lights, and bar top all interplay, and reinforce, the darker more intimate setting of the Eberly Dining Room, while the Study is gritty and industrial. Blackened steel structures, rough-troweled plaster walls, and industrial brass light fixtures help to serve to transition guests between spaces.

The Cedar Tavern is a mixture of the two. Refined touches include the ornate woodwork of the bar, jade mosaic hex floor, concrete tile wainscot, and brass light fixtures. Gritty counterpoints include exposed concrete and steel beams, blackened steel, and the grit inherent in a 100-plus-year-old bar salvaged from Cedar Tavern in Greenwich Village.

Subtle threads link the distinct spaces, though each offers guests a different version of the Eberly experience. The visual transparency between all spaces in conjunction with juxtaposed interiors culminate to create a unique experience under one roof.

La Cabra

Location / Madrid, Spain

Completion / 2018

Area / 1,410 square feet (131 square meters)

Client / Javier Aranda

Design / mecanismo

Photography / Kavi Sánchez

An architecture studio located in Madrid, mecanismo was founded by Marta Urtasun and Pedro Rica, two young architects with a dynamic and different vision of architecture and its processes. The studio has achieved a unique line of work, directly associated to the importance of details and conceptual innovation. Today, its team of young professionals specialize in the design, development, and execution of projects, systems and architectural products.

○ The space

The use of space in this Michelin-starred restaurant was completely changed. Designers transformed the space by removing all partitions and opening up spaces that were previously divided into different sections, concentrating users into one specific area instead of taking advantage of all the space. They created a single unique homogenous area in which all the new prefabricated elements were placed. Each functional space is linked to a different architectural element, designed by the mecanismo team.

○ The flow

The new pieces and the removal of all partitions created a new sense of flow in the space. The entrance is only the starting point of the space

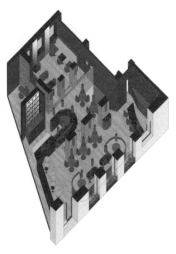

Three-dimensional plan

where the user chooses their own itinerary. The new architecture elements offer a variety of options for the user to choose and move around in the space.

Designers wanted to create a space that provided optimum utilization for users (both wait staff and guests) to be able to move freely while maintaining an efficient circulation.

(Before) (After)

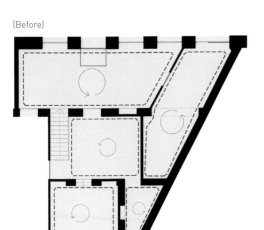
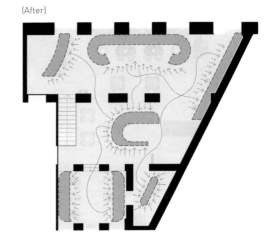

Functional areas

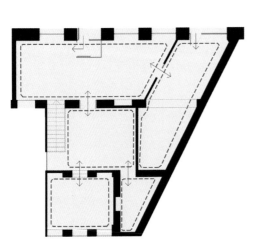
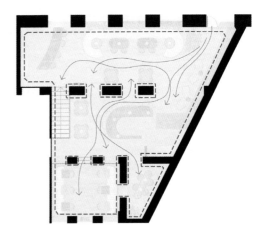

The flow

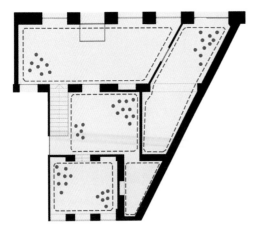
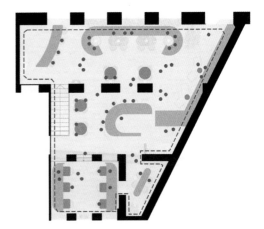

Spatial density

○ Decoration

When designers were asked to do the project, the condition was that the restaurant would only be closed for three weeks. After that time, they had confirmed reservations. For that reason, the works had to be done during a strict and short period of time. The first part took place before the three weeks and consisted of the design and production of most of the elements. The second part was the actual intervention, which lasted three weeks, and involved installing prefabricated elements and the space modifications.

The prefabricated elements included bars, tables, sofas, lamps, and chairs. Everything (except for the chairs) was designed by the mecanismo team based on the same concept, using a wooden walnut brick pattern. Wood is combined with other natural materials like marble for eating surfaces, steel was used in auxiliary elements, and fabric upholstered all the sofas and chair seats.

(Before)

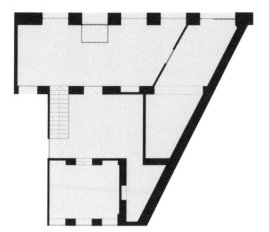

(After)

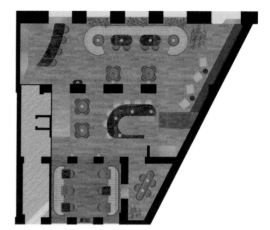

Floor plan

When the intervention site date came, most of the work had been done, and elements were ready to be installed. The team spent most of the three weeks creating the new space distribution, covering the structure walls using bricks and painting the ceilings. At the same time, they installed prefabricated elements in the space.

○ Design elements

Lighting was one of the most important aspects in the project, a way to create a new and warm atmosphere. Dim, soft, and indirect lighting was used. In order to get this ambiance, the team designed two kinds of suspended lamps using the same concept and materials as in the rest of the elements.

Designers used several homogenous and neutral colors in order to focus the architectural elements. The use of neutral colors provides a more calming atmosphere as well as creating a backdrop for details in the space.

Miss Wong

Location / Laval, Quebec, Canada
Completion / 2018
Area / 10,000 square feet (929 square meters)

Client / Miss Wong
Design / Ménard Dworkind Architecture & Design
Photography / David Dworkind

Ménard Dworkind Architecture & Design is a Montreal-based firm founded in 2017 through the union of Atelier Mainor and David Dworkind Architecture. They specialize in commercial interiors, residential architecture, and industrial design. They thrive on detail-oriented spaces in which each element relates to a central narrative to create a cohesive experience that resonates with the users. This level of coherence is achieved by giving the same attention to the big ideas as to the smallest details.

○ The space

The main area of the restaurant breaks off into four different zones that surround it. These areas are smaller and more intimate. Each of them has its own unique characteristics, allowing people a different dining experience every time they visit. The design uses risers to play with different heights to create this effect of zones. The ground level is the largest zone subdivided into the red zone where walls, floor, and furniture are all in red and is topped by hundreds of red Chinese lanterns. The main space was planned as a beer garden with long communal tables at bar height where the party picks up and converts to a dance floor late at night.

Tucked away behind the stair is a zone which has lower couch seating around vintage coffee tables found in Montreal's Chinatown and has

(Before)

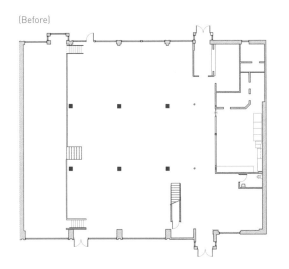

(After)

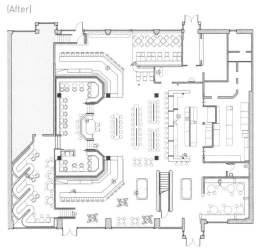

Plan

an opium den–inspired vibe. The walls are covered in square wooden panels with Chinese engravings that were recovered from a closed Chinese restaurant. Compared to the vastness of the main space, this space with low ceilings and lower couches and tables creates a more intimate atmosphere.

The beer-garden space is flanked by two symmetrical segmented L-shaped bars that hug the first riser. Banquette seating surrounds the first riser where tables can be put together for groups of all sizes. The top riser is subdivided by a curved banquette that comes off the wall at 45 degrees, creating a dynamic seating area for groups, couples, or individuals to overlook the action below.

○ **The flow**

The user enters the restaurant under a low ceiling and passes through a vintage Chinese arch framing a portrait of Miss Wong herself. This compressed space then opens up into the main area of the restaurant, which is an enormous 10,000 square feet (929 square meters) with 22-foot-tall (7-meter-tall) ceilings.

○ **Decoration**

Much of the furniture and lighting is bespoke and is a contemporary take on Chinese design. The communal tables are topped with library lights custom made out of powder-coated, laser-cut steel, with Mandarin characters that read "I don't speak Chinese." At the convergence of these communal tables is a VIP booth covered in red velour that surrounds a table in Rosso Levanto marble.

Lights reflect off the custom walnut tables, creating an uplit warm glow on peoples' faces. Long steel tubes curve off the railing of the first riser, creating a vaulted effect over the bar, and end in a hook hanging yellow lanterns over the bar. These were inspired by Chinese fishermens' lanterns.

The bar lights over the kitchen are a smaller version of the lights over the bar, replicating the asymmetrical curved steel tubes with smaller lanterns.

Many of the chairs were salvaged and re-upholstered, while the bar stools were inexpensive and sturdy workshop stools that were repainted in a dark green to match the ceiling.

The color palette is mostly comprised of red and green commonly found in restaurants around Chinatown. There is a contrast with raw steel elements such as the scissor gate handrails that flank the risers and staircase.

○ **Design elements**

After a few days visiting the Chinatowns of San Francisco and Vancouver, the architect-designer team Guillaume Ménard and David Dworkind developed a clear design intention for the Miss Wong restaurant in Laval. They were inspired by the vibrant neon signage, the classic folding scissor gates, and the hanging lanterns, all of which created a bright and exciting atmosphere.

Hanging on the columns are six large neon and lightbox signs advertising fictional shops. These signs, and the custom lamps on the tables, create a street-market ambiance. Custom-designed lights and stools give the space an entirely unique character.

Numnum

Location / Ankara, Turkey

Completion / 2015

Area / 4,252 square feet (395 square meters)

Client / İstanbul Yiyecek İçecek Grubu

Design / Ofist

Photography / Ali Bekman

Ofist was founded in 2004 by the interior architects and designers Yasemin Arpac and Sabahattin Emir in Istanbul. The partners focus on creating designs with the responsibility and awareness of being a part of a city which still embodies the profound traces of different cultures who inhabited the metropolis over many centuries still evident on its streets, squares, buildings, and citizens.

○ The space

This was one of nine Numnum restaurants in Turkey. Since the whole structure was produced from scratch over a platform that was an annex to a shopping mall, the whole layout was planned for the perfect circulation and function. Considering the changing nature of smoking regulations, all interior spaces were designed to be open-air, free-smoking areas when desired. Depending on the weather conditions, all dining areas can act as outdoor or indoor spaces.

An open plan placed the kitchen at one corner, while a bar subsuming the pizza oven takes a more central location to make easy access for drinks services and create a lively, bustling environment.

The needed dimensions for the kitchen and bar areas were designated at the first stage. All the dining areas were scattered around and in

(Before)

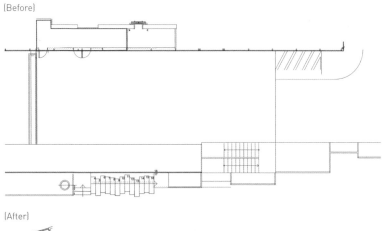

(After)

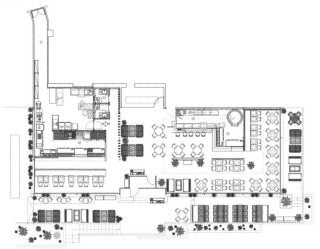

Plan

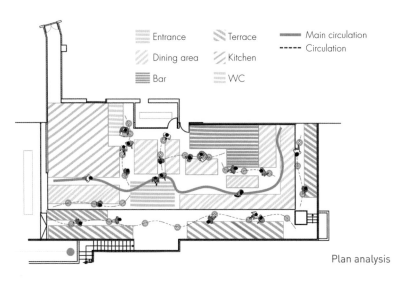

Entrance ▦ Terrace ▨ ▬ Main circulation
Dining area ▨ Kitchen ▨ ---- Circulation
Bar ▤ WC ▦

Plan analysis

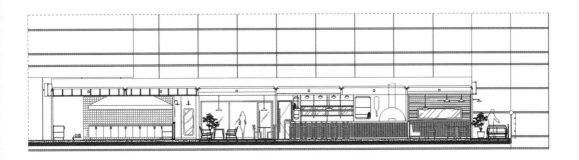

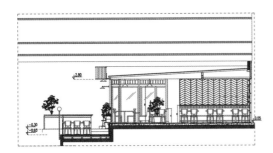
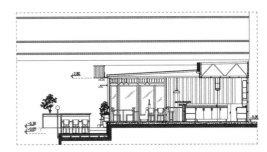

Sections

between, creating small gatherings of people, avoiding masses of tables. As this is one of Numnum's smallest restaurants, the effectiveness of all these areas was crucial, allowing as much seating as possible.

○ Decoration and design

While developing a flow between all dining spaces, the groups of seating create slightly different feelings with the use of various furniture pieces. Alternate seating heights, different types of chairs, and garden-style seating elements among indoor furniture, are all used together to create a dynamic and fun social space.

This dynamic feeling is also achieved with the use of various colors and materials. To create a warm, familiar and more homey feeling to the users, different types of wood are used around the same space. These woods also differ in surface treatments with the use of colors or varnishes. Pine, iroko, beech, and oak are used in various elements as well as plywood.

Metal is also widely used around the restaurant, both in decorative elements and furniture. Black or white painted iron elements act as separators, hangers, bearing systems for some storing, or display in units. Colorful Tolix chairs are scattered around, along with some custom-made metal lounge chairs, and sofas with colorful cushions.

This dynamism also continues in the lighting elements. Different materials like brass, iron, and glass are all used around the same space. The small black-and-white hexagonal floor tiles create a warm, cozy, and fun feeling, which becomes even warmer together with iroko decks and parquet. Black, white, and light gray marble is also used for some counters and tabletops.

Populist Bebek

Location / Istanbul, Turkey

Completion / 2018

Area / 4,521 square feet (420 square meters)

Client / d.ream

Design / Lagranja Design

Photography / Ali Bekman

Designing at Lagranja has always been a matter of ideas, not ideology. The staff do not sit at the drafting table with a pre-made list of what they should or what they should not do. They believe each project is unique and has to be approached in a different way. They try to understand the context, they ask themselves and their clients many questions, they draw a strategy, and they look for the right tools and the appropriate team. And they let things be.

○ The space

The Populist restaurant is located in the former space of a garden villa, in Bebek, a neighborhood situated on the Bosphorus strait. In order to fit the neighborhood's characteristics and to offer people a different user experience, a refined and dreamy look has been created.

The space comprises a basement kitchen; first floor with garden, terrace, bar, bathroom, and storage area; and second floor with restaurant, another bar, and more bathrooms.

○ The flow

The main aim was to connect the ample exterior space with the interior, as well as opening the first floor to the second floor. The space can be

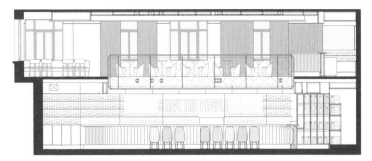

Section

accessed through several entrances located on the outdoor terrace. The
bar is placed in a way that gives flow to the circulation. Everything can be
seen and people can interact with the space; they can take a seat right
from the moment they step in, go to the bar, or chat and dance around the
tables in the middle of the space. The staircase that gives access to the
quieter spaces on the first floor is located near the entrance, but placed

in a way that is not intrusive to the space. Upstairs, the layout guides the diners to their seat, where they can enjoy their meal while still being able to take a look at the people downstairs. It was important to maintain a strong connection between the two floors and allow people upstairs to still have fun and feel the atmosphere even while they are eating.

○ **Dividing the space**

Designers did not want to create an enclosed space using partition walls or any vertical divisions. The aim was to think about the restaurant as an open, homogeneous space with the help of three main ingredients: the textures, the furniture, and the two floors. Therefore, the area divisions are made by the change in materials, both in the pavement and in the wall covering and the furniture configuration, as well as the geometry of the bar and the opening of the first floor. The aim was to ensure a lot of space around the tables for people to dance or gather around while enjoying drinks and snacks. The bar is a single elongated curve that allows customers to be served from various points. With the help of these elements, the users are moving in a certain way inside the space and the group of people created becomes an organic space divider.

(Before)

(After)

Second-floor plan

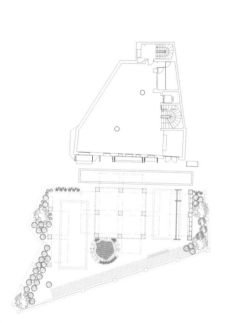

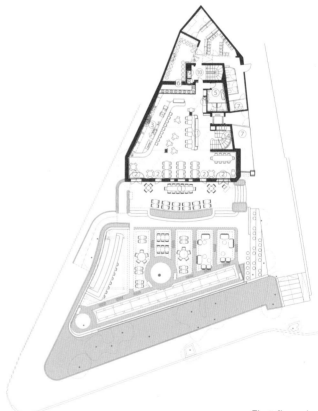

① Terrace
② Entrance
③ Bar counter
④ Staircase
⑤ Toilets
⑥ Kegs fridge
⑦ Machine room
⑧ Electric room
⑨ Service elevator
⑩ Emergency stairs
⑪ Service station

First-floor plan

○ Dimensions

At the beginning, the two existing floors had more or less the same dimensions. From the start, it was very important not only to divide the spaces, but to unify them. It was clear for designers that they would need to make an intervention that would change the proportions of the space and the dynamics of the restaurant. The decision to make a cut in the middle of the first floor was made with the aim of vertically connecting the two levels. Nevertheless, it was crucial to maintain a certain balance between the first floor where people are constantly moving and the upper floor where people are mostly seated and eating their meals. The goal was to create a dreamy scenario where people can have fun, so this decision allowed the designers to install the Beer Dream Machine. The installation is a ceiling-mounted sculptural piece that serves as lighting and simulates the circuit of beer fabrication. As the second floor became a balcony overlooking the main level, the Beer Dream Machine vertically connects the area and allows people to see it from every point of the restaurant.

○ Decoration

Decorative elements included wall coverings made of salmon and green lacquered metallic stripes combined with glass stripes. Bespoke furniture was constructed, including oak and marble tabletops and a reclaimed oak bar, along with salmon and green chairs and stools.

○ Design elements

Two years before Populist Bebek was opened, Lagranja Design studio had converted Turkey's first beer company into a modern brewery-restaurant

with an industrial look, inspired by the graphic language of the Prohibition period. The result was the original Populist, located in the Bomonti area of Istanbul. In creating the second restaurant for the same brand, the designers were working in a space with some distinct characteristics that demanded new ideas and solutions, and could not just adapt the original design. Taking into consideration that the beer served in the restaurant is made in the first Populist, the design team was inspired to come up with a key element in the design: the Beer Dream Machine.

Other important elements that contribute to the overall visual effects of the restaurant are the neon signs. They recall the disobedient atmosphere created during Prohibition times. Protest is reflected in a

tangible yet fun aesthetic, using slogans related to food and beverage.
The bold messages are ironic and humorous, with messages such as
"Hands off my glass," "Fight for your fries," and "Burger is the answer."
The white light was chosen for the neon to make the text noticeable
without being overwhelming, so the emphasis is kept on the overall
space. The slogans almost act like paintings that add dynamism to
the design and make the user feel as if they are stepping in a friendly
environment. This element, already present in the first premises
Lagranja designed for Populist, is the only one repeated in order to give
consistency to the brand.

Restaurant "Holy moly!"

Location / Moscow, Russia
Completion / 2017
Area / 1,561 square feet (145 square meters)

Client / Restaurant "Holy moly!"
Design / Kristina Uspenieva
Photography / Mikhail Chekalov

Kristina Uspenieva was born in Kazakhstan, and has lived and studied in Krasnoyarsk and Moscow. She has a legal education, and has worked as a stylist, coming to interior design out of a desire to work on a larger scale. She focuses on private residences and apartments, as well as designing for the hospitality industry (restaurants and hotels), recreation centers, and childcare facilities.

○ The space

The restaurant is designed for people traveling down one of the main roads of Russia. Guests stop to take a break, have a snack, or take some food with them. They may stop for breakfast or even to celebrate a special event.

The building itself was designed more than 10 years before this re-fit, and nothing had changed since then. Roadside restaurants are not generally considered significant or interesting, but in this case the designer wanted to bring a light, airy feel to the space, increase the seating capacity, and make the guest experience more pleasant, offering a place to feel comfortable after a trip. She wanted to create a clean interior with active colors, take advantage of the multicolor wall, and add retro touches.

○ The flow

The restaurant is located on the first floor, but the space also includes a second-floor balcony that was turned into a lounge area with comfortable sofas. The accent in the hall is the bar counter, which emphasizes the height of the space. The tables are arranged in a range of configurations so that guests will find a convenient option for themselves, whether it's two people or a large party.

The space is divided into two zones and there was an opportunity to put a large oval table not far from the entrance, with space for 10 people. High-back sofas allow guests to talk peacefully with each other. The balcony with lounge area is clearly visible from the bar counter and is accessed via a central staircase that passes through the entire building.

(Before)

(After)

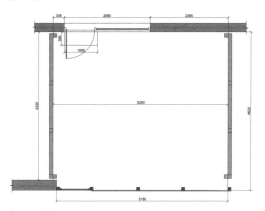

Second-floor plan

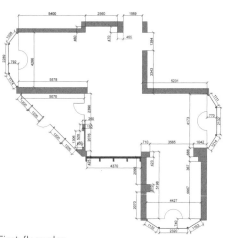

First-floor plan

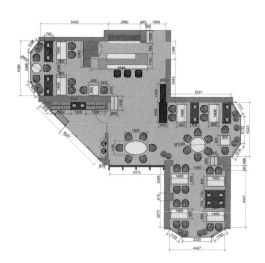

The hall, restaurant, lounge and staircase are reflected in a series of mirrors that bind the spaces visually, allowing them to flow from one to another.

The bar counter is the center of the composition, a vertical line that holds everything else together. The halls have low ceilings, while the bar area has a double-height space. The walls and ceilings were painted in the same color as the bar counter, giving the room an additional sense of spaciousness.

○ **Decoration**

Everything was designed specifically for this project. Brass lamps, upholstered furniture, wardrobes, and the bar counter were made by local craftsmen according to the designer's sketches.

○ **Design elements**

It is a double-height space, and the bar counter was raised higher, adding more height to the room. The designer chose to retain a bas-relief on the wall, made with a metal frame, plaster, and paint. Fresh paint was added, and the wall has become an appealing accent.

The tabletops are made of varnished poplar, with small copies of the tables and chairs available for children.

The Commons

Location / Maastricht, the Netherlands

Completion / 2018

Area / 10,495 square feet (975 square meters)

Client / The Student Hotel & The Commons

Design / Studio Modijefsky

Photography / Maarten Willemstein

Studio Modijefsky is an interior architecture studio founded by Esther Stam in 2009. Its home in the center of Amsterdam hosts an international team of architects and interior designers who provide creative spatial interventions services for clients, ranging from hotels to boutiques and bars to spas. The eight women that currently form the studio carefully design everything that is seen, passed, and touched by a visitor for the duration of their stay whether it's for five seconds or five hours.

It's part of the studio's ultimate goal to reinvent the way people interact with an interior. By relating design to the location's context (whether natural or urban) and playing with the composition of texture and materials, light and routing, height and depth, sight, and tactility, Studio Modijefsky creates spatial experiences that surpass all expectations and create valuable new memories.

The past years have led to a project list containing interior projects in the Netherlands and abroad, such as Bar Botanique, Kanarie Club, Wyers, and The Commons.

○ The space

Across three levels, The Commons restaurant and bar has a bold and vibrant interior, celebrating the heritage of both the site and the production process that used to take place in the old Sphinx ceramics factory.

Designed to serve as both the breakfast area of the attached hotel and an all-day bar and dining space, this light-filled restaurant with an industrial edge easily adapts to both.

The first level incorporates the entrance, main area, bar, restaurant, kitchen, active area, and breakfast buffet. On the mezzanine level is the lounge restaurant, service point, and active area. The basement provides a flexible space for chilling out and events, as well as another bar and active area, and toilets.

Situated in the steel-constructed, north-east corner of the building is a very prominent new addition, grabbing your attention and inviting you in with its distinctive 16-foot-high (5-meter-high) logo adorning the glass façade.

○ **The flow**

All levels of the restaurant are linked together by conceptual elevators—leather daybeds in various shapes and colors, suspended on metal rails. This playful reference is a nod towards the horizontal skyscraper theme

and encourages people to use the restaurant more freely through a clever placement of chill-out furniture.

To divide the space, designers opened up the building, using pillars, the central bar, and open kitchen, with enough space in the back for employees, storage and so on.

A dark steel bar framed by two symmetrical staircases takes center stage.

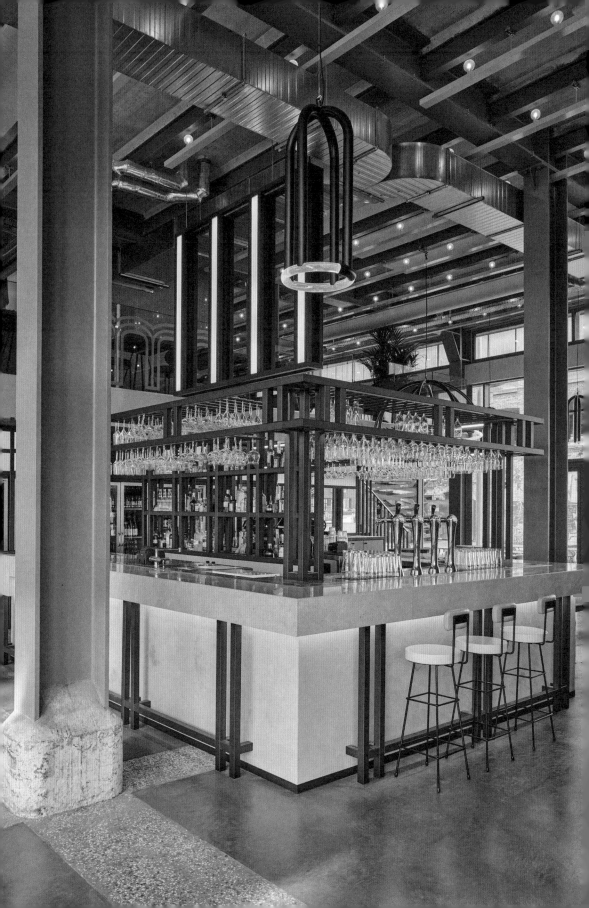

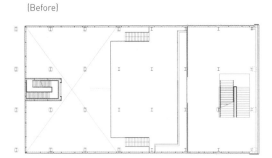

Mezzanine plan

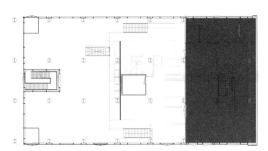
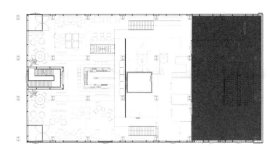

First-floor plan

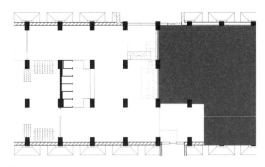
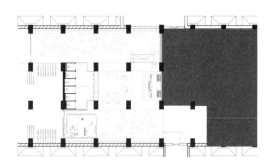

Basement plan

○ Decoration

The bespoke furniture and refined color scheme of the interior are inspired by the ceramic production process. Pastel shades of blue, gray, pink, and yellow in the basement refer to the start of the process, using water and clay with round, geometrical footstools reflecting the shapes of pottery molds. The first floor is kept in slightly brighter tones of freshly glazed pottery. The mezzanine was designed using the most intense tones resembling finely baked ceramics. The pottery theme is continued with a variety of custom-made round tables and the use of the lazy susan, taking their distinct shapes from pottery wheels and work benches. The process of baking is referenced in the basement, where bathrooms are covered in dark tiles resemble burnt ovens, with cylindrical lights appearing above them like a roaring fire.

○ Design elements

The designers believe that each space should have its own unique identity. They develop this identity by collecting a lot of information on the history of the space, the spatial qualities, the context of the space, and what it will host. Based on all this information, a concept was developed and then translated into an interior design.

For example, in the mezzanine, a bright and cozy space is filled with custom-made tables, and banquet seats is located above the kitchen. The basement, connected to the first floor by a dark steel staircase, is designed to hold events such as concerts, poetry nights, and book readings.

Ward With V dots

Location / Taipei, Taiwan, China

Completion / 2018

Area / 1,628 square feet (151 square meters)

Client / Ward With V dots

Design / B+P Architects

Photography / Studio Millspace

B+P Architects is a professional space design team across business industries, carrying out each step from concept and preliminary design to detail design and construction, creating brand-new living environments and building spaces with mixed materials and areas.

○ **The space**

The original space is an old hospital, redesigned to be used as a restaurant space and factory for bean products. The space was separated by columns between ward beds and a central walkway. After planning, columns in the original space were maintained by the designer. The white box on the right is used as the bean-making area, while the space on the left becomes a commodity display area and a dining area.

○ **The flow**

People enter the atrium from the right entrance. The client has plans to set up a charity shop in the future, so the designer decided to remove a

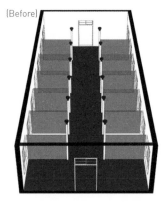

(Before)

(After)

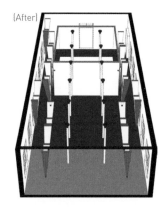

Ward in a hospital

Floor space of restaurant

frontage window to set up a new entrance, making it convenient for people to enter and exit and promoting the commercial value of the shop.

The first view on entering the space is a white box space that the visitor can walk around and see the entire process of making bean products, from picking, grinding, and extracting beans to making beans into soybean milk, tofu pudding, and tofu skin, to cooling and packaging

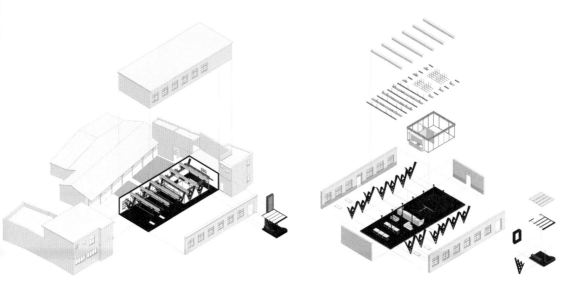

Axonometric

products. The exterior of the box space is framed by a V framework to attract customers to stop and look.

After being guided around the box space, customers can enter the dining area and the merchandise area at the back, or go to other areas, such as the workshop and the youth hostel, through the atrium.

The original columns in the space are used to support the framework now, and define the space. The design is embedded with a new structural system, "V dots," which act as structures, partitions, inner windows, furniture, exhibition booths, and light fixtures. The central walkway of the ward rooms has become the new center of the space, and the V framework can separate the seats in the restaurant from the service area.

The original rectangular ward room is divided by two rows of columns into a central walkway and two zones for ward beds, so the designer sets the V-shaped column based on the size and location of columns in the original space. The staggered arrangement of the original column and the V-shaped column forms the dining area, the decoration area, the walkway, and the bean-making house space.

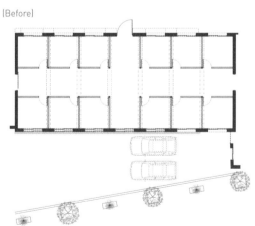

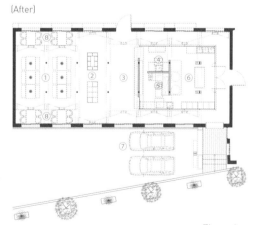

Floor plan

① Dining area
② Goods display
③ Counter
④ Select area
⑤ Packaging area
⑥ Production area
⑦ Parking
⑧ Office

○ **Decoration**

The designer wanted to create a new space that could combine the new and the old, so white iron columns, white walls, and gray concrete floors of the original space have been maintained. The overall background of the space presents a light gray tone, while new furniture uses pure black and white to make a contrast. The black V framework, as the most important element in the space, is also seen as part of the furniture—the display cabinet, the table frame, the screen, and the light fixture. In terms of materials, metal has been used as a response to the original columns. The color of the bean-making house, floors, and walls are gray, making a strong contrast with the bean-making equipment made of stainless steel.

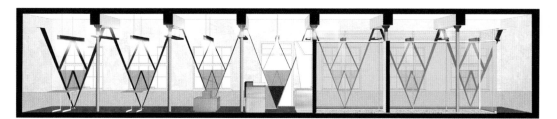

Section

○ **Design elements**

Windows and columns within the original space delineate a new structure that forms an atrium and a walkway. At the same time, the segmentation of old window and glass texture has been retained. The old window, walkway, blue-dyed curtain and white box create a unique visual experience from outside.

Birch Residence

Location / Los Angeles, United States
Completion / 2015
Area / 3,600 square feet (334 square meters)

Client / Birch Family
Design / Griffin Enright Architects
Photography / Benny Chan Photoworks

Griffin Enright Architects is an award-winning, interdisciplinary Los Angeles–based firm with institutional, cultural, and residential projects built nationally and abroad. Griffin Enright Architects was founded by Margaret Griffin and John Enright as a collaborative design practice that explores new prospects for the built environment through their integration of architectural, urban, landscape, and interior design. Using focused, inventive, and strategic thinking, they pursue unexpected solutions to transform overlooked conditions into landmark projects through their expertise in construction techniques and community engagement.

○ **The space**

The Birch house is designed with a semi-subterranean garage to enlarge the garden oasis at the back. The contrast between private and open areas is obvious throughout the entire building.

On the first floor the living room, dining, kitchen, and family room are open to the curvilinear skylight, the glass bridge, and glass curtain wall. The connection to the skylight and curtain wall connects the different programs in the living room, as well as visually driving the space into the back yard. In contrast, the bathrooms, guest bedroom, and the main office remain more private and enclosed for privacy. The gym and a secondary office are placed in the accessory building next to the backyard and the pool, as part of the more public and flexible program.

The second floor is dedicated to the bedrooms of the house. Both bedrooms have a connection to the outside; they each have an extended private terrace which creates a seamless connection between inside and outside.

○ **The flow**

The house is organized around a curvilinear path that navigates through the residence, accentuating the narrowness of the lot, and connecting the public and private areas of the site. This path is a central vertical atrium that creates the entry, a connection to the sky above, and leads to the garden and pool which is engaged directly into the house. The slight curvatures of the walls allow for glimpses of views within the house and runs vertically through a 50-foot-long (15-meter-long) skylight, while a glass bridge connects the two upper bedroom wings.

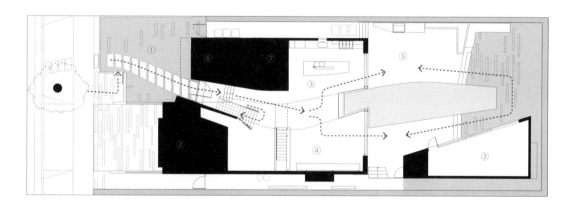

1. Garden
2. Office
3. Kitchen
4. Living
5. Outdoor living
6. Bathroom
7. Bedroom
8. Deck
9. Roof garden
10. WC
11. Closet

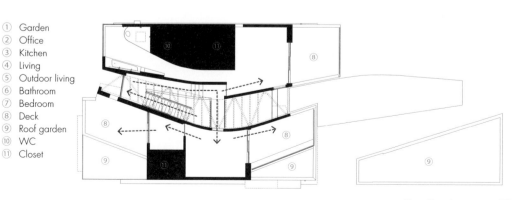

Functional areas and flow

As one moves through the entry, the vertical space expands on the first floor to form an open glass area which is the full width of the house, opening to the private exterior garden, decks and pool. Translucent wall and skylight panels diffuse the southern light, and are lit from within for evening lighting.

The sculptural staircase is both connected to the house and floating within it, while the transparent glass bridge in the second floor hovers in the void above, transmitting multiple lighting effects and connecting both wings. The void acts as a circulation guide which bisects the space and moves from space to space, from outside to inside, and from public to private to create a house where the inhabitants are actively engaged in a sinuous and fluid form of spatial interaction.

Visual connection to the yard throughout the entire house is an important concept of the residence; therefore glass is used as a major space divider between spaces for the open programs. The curvilinear skylight and glass curtain wall not only bring natural daylight into the house but also create expanded views. The more private programs are enclosed and sheltered by solid material. The void also plays an important role in the geometry of the house; the void embraces the curved geometry to reconnect the apparent space.

(Before)

(After)

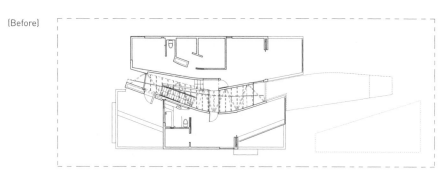

Second-floor plan

(Before)

(After)

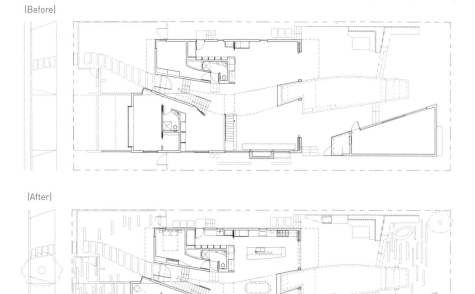

First-floor plan

○ Dimensions

The residence has either visual or physical connections to the exterior; the program is compact, yet designed to create a sense of expanded volume. A double-story central volume curves through the house, creating extended views and maximizing daylight from the skylight and sunshade above. The backyard has a courtyard feel and a curved pool which echoes the form of the central volume, drawing attention through the house.

○ Design elements

The elongated skylight points toward east and west, and provides constant natural daylight and sunlight for the house along with the glass curtain wall. The use of transparency also establishes visual connection from inside to outside in various points of the project. The hall becomes a viewing device, allowing for both internal and external connections. Movement occurs along the curve, converging and diverging at threshold moments, creating sinuous pathways that are punctuated by city views, framed within the vertical slot of space.

Frame House

Location / Upper Thomson, Singapore

Completion / 2015

Area / 2,056 square feet (191 square meters)

Design / Atelier M+A

Photography / Robert Such, Masaki Harimoto

Atelier M+A is an architectural and interior design studio headed by Masaki Harimoto and Ng Ai Hwa since 2009. The atelier emphasizes professionalism and quality for every project. Atelier M+A constantly explores design possibilities and challenges design constraints. Collectively, the design brief, site, and program are analyzed and considered to achieve design authenticity for each project.

○ **The space**

The project was the transformation of a 50-year-old dilapidated terrace house in Singapore. The drive for the design was to bring in natural light and natural ventilation to the deep and dim interior, which is the result of typical mass-developed housing projects in Singapore.

The challenge of the project was to achieve a sense of spaciousness for a house situated in a narrow piece of land, while fulfilling the living functions for the owner's family of four and their maid.

Designers planned for the first story to be a space for the common living space, primarily comprising of the living room, dining area, and kitchen. These were fitted within a combined open space without partitions. An adjacent multipurpose room with sliding door panels was plugged in beside the living space to allow as an extension of space during

gatherings, or as a separate guest room or activity room when the need arises.

The sense of spaciousness at the first story is enhanced as it opens to the front patio and internal courtyard. One could view from the patio all the way to the kitchen situated at the rear. The living, dining, and kitchen areas and the inner courtyard connect seamlessly, with the sense of space further extending toward the sky from the inner courtyard.

The second and the third stories were kept for private spaces; essentially the bedrooms and bathrooms. An alcove space was carved out of the third-story corridor to allow a study corner for the owner.

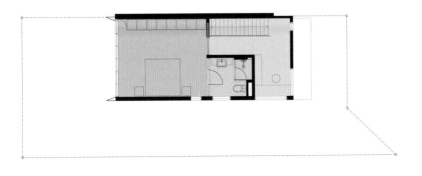

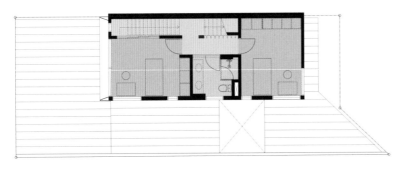

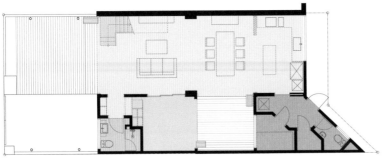

Common living space
Multi-purpose room
Bathroom
Stair / Corridor
Utility
Bedrooms

Zoning plans

(Before)

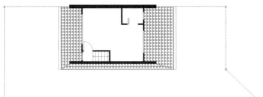

(After)

Third-floor plan

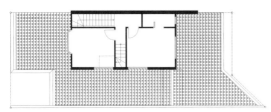

Second-floor plan

First-floor plan

① Car porch
② Patio
③ Living
④ Dining
⑤ Kitchen
⑥ Guest bath
⑦ Multi-purpose room
⑧ Internal courtyard
⑨ Utility
⑩ Maid's room
⑪ Store
⑫ Bath
⑬ Bedroom
⑭ Void
⑮ Roof
⑯ Master bedroom
⑰ Master bath
⑱ Study room

○ **The flow**

A straight flight of stairs with a high-volume stairwell connects all floors and creates a vertical continuity within the house. With the house sitting on a narrow, long piece of land, the staircase is planned in a linear manner aligning to the wall to avoid the circulation space from invading further into the compact interior space.

Section

The introduction of an internal open-to-sky courtyard is the most important feature of the Frame House in introducing natural daylight and in generating natural ventilation, both critical factors for the tropical climate. The inner courtyard enhances the opportunity to introduce cross ventilation and natural light to deep corners of the house.

○ Design elements

Sandwiched among the grim terrace housing estate, the house directs and frames one's viewpoint toward the interior space within. The frame on the front façade and around windows wards off rain effectively, and is painted in black as a contrast from the white walls to accentuate the framing effect. Windows are carefully positioned not only to bring in light but also to frame views of the sky and greenery.

WH Residence

Location / Odessa, Ukraine

Completion / 2017

Area / 7,965 square feet (740 square meters)

Design / M3 Architects

Photography / Antony Garets, Illia Temnov

M3 Architects specializes in the creation of private and commercial facilities, which are comfortable and functional spaces for life, work, and leisure. Its worldview is a tool for liquidation of everything superfluous in favor of focusing on the most important things in life. The key point of the firm's philosophy is to achieve maximum signal and minimum noise. Where the signal is important information and the noise is extraneous.

○ The space

All functional areas are divided into three groups—private, public, and technical areas. The common space is located on the first floor. An entrance, wardrobes, a living room, and a kitchen with a dining area compose a public space. Technical rooms are located on the same floor as a separate block. The space of the first floor is visually combined with the yard and the pool area; compositionally both volumes are open to each other and form a common space. The first floor acts as a base, and allows the circulation of air and natural light through the building. The front door, and the living room with a kitchen and dining area are established on the same level to achieve the most convenient and open layout for the first floor. The open transparent volume of a staircase leads to the second and third floors, where the private areas are located.

(Before)

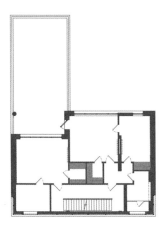
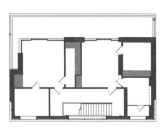

① Hall
② Studio-kitchen
③ Wardrobe
④ Utility room
⑤ Toilet
⑥ Terrace
⑦ Bedroom
⑧ Cabinet
⑨ Corridor

(After)

First-floor plan   Second-floor plan   Third-floor plan

The bedrooms are established like separate units with bathrooms and wardrobes. Each bedroom has an exit to the terrace with a view to the courtyard.

○ The flow

The first floor is the main volume, performing the role of the base of the composition with conventional borders, and is filled with air and warm light. To achieve the most convenient and open layout of the first-level spaces, the entrance from the street is situated on the same plane as the pool area, veranda and the living room on the other side of the section, and the entrance group and the exit to the terrace from the living room are located in different parts of the buildings, providing privacy to the owners.

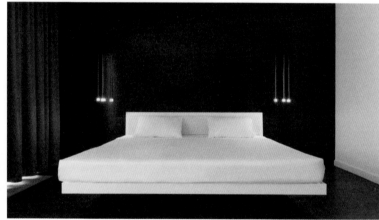

○ **Design elements**

The residence is located in Odessa, Ukraine, near the Black Sea coastal area. The neighborhood of Arcadia is the main resort area in Ukraine, and is a main clubbing center of the country. The residence is erected from structures of two houses. Both buildings contain the same number of functions. The main façades of these two buildings are combined into a composition and oriented to a luxury apartment house. The buildings are equipped with solar collectors that provide energy for heating pools, back-up boilers, ventilation and air-conditioning systems. The key factor for architectural solutions for the residence was to create the most open but private space of two separate symmetrical volumes in conditions of a dense urban environment.

Hotel Adriatic

Location / Rovinj, Croatia
Completion / 2014
Area / 20,570 square feet (1,911 square meters)

Client / Maistra d.d.
Design / 3LHD
Photography / Domagoj Blažević, Siniša Gulić, Ognjen Maravić, SofijaSilvia, Duško Vlaović, Jure Živković

3LHD is an architectural practice focused on integrating various disciplines–architecture, urban planning, design, and art. The studio was founded in Zagreb in 1994 by four partners: Saša Begović, Marko Dabrović, Tatjana Grozdanić Begović, and Silvije Novak. In 2016 they appointed a new partner, Paula Kukuljica.

○ **The space**

The existing building situated on an attractive site next to the sea was constructed in 1913 as one of the first hotels in the region. The hotel building is located in the protected historic center of Rovinj, which meant the renovation project had to work within strict conservation parameters. The guidelines were fully abided by, and full reconstruction of the façade was implemented without any modern reinterpretation.

Changes were allowed in the interior, with reconstruction plans based on spacious rooms, and first-floor catering facilities oriented to outside guests as well as hotel guests. A series of interventions opened up the interior, with emphasis placed on maintaining the existing staircase that leads from the first to the fourth floor. The placement of the new staircase from the first floor to the rooms was designed to open the public hotel amenities, the café and brasserie, toward the town square.

Each area in the hotel was treated individually and has a different atmosphere: the brasserie is comfortable, in Mediterranean shades, while black hallways are illuminated by artistic light installations leading to white and airy rooms overlooking the urban life of the old town.

Croatian artist SofijaSilvia and Slovenian artist Jasmina Cibic designed works for the brasserie and café-bar. Atmospheric photographs of the Golden Cape and Rovinj archipelago by SofijaSilvia reveal the dreams of an adventurous traveler; for guests looking at the fairy-tale scenery in the photographs, while surrounded by the hotel interior evoking various historical periods, their view extends from the Mediterranean hotel terrace onto the archipelago islands and landscapes beyond.

Spacious bright rooms are like artist studios; their intimate ambiance provides a feeling of an elegant home instead of a hotel room. Room sizes vary, furnished similarly but containing completely different works of art. French artist Abdelkader Benchamma created drawings on the spot, directly on room walls, in clean and intense lines, inviting guests into a melancholic and dreamy vision of the universe and its natural phenomena. Croatian artist Igor Eškinja uses a subtle and elegant approach in the almost forgotten photography technique of cyanotype, letting sunlight "paint" on a photosensitive emulsion.

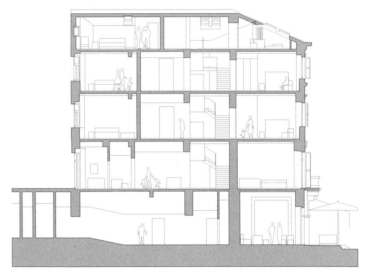

Section

The most luxurious room in the hotel has a unique view from two balconies, a freestanding bathtub by the bed, and oil on canvas by the Croatian painter Zlatan Vehabović. White rooms are entered into from spacious black corridors containing artworks dealing with various aspects of light by Italian artist Massimo Uberti. A light installation in the shape of a door invites the observer to play with their own imagination; imagine the worlds residing in this hotel area before numerous renovations and changing with passing times that left subtle traces.

An artistic installation by Austrian artist Valentin Ruhry is almost 50 feet (15 meters) high and passes through and connects with the old hotel staircase, the only area of the interior maintaining its original form in the century-old building. The geometrically abstract composition of rectangular lines carries fluorescent tubes and provides light to the area. Two vertically set steel props extend from the middle of the window pane at the top of the staircase all the way to the beginning of its spiral, achieving intertwined traditional architectural and modern trans-disciplinary artistic expression.

○ **Design elements**

By a comprehensive reconstruction and a collective effort of creative artists from Croatia, Slovenia, Austria, Italy, Germany, and France, gathered around 3LHD's concept, the hotel was transformed into

(Before)   (After)

Third-floor plan

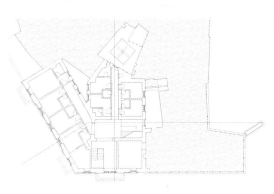   

Second-floor plan

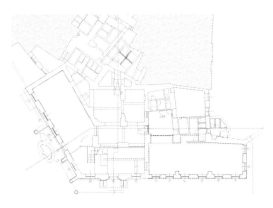   

First-floor plan

① Hotel entrance
② Cafe entrance
③ Brasserie entrance
④ Reception
⑤ Café
⑥ Brasserie
⑦ Toilet
⑧ Service bar
⑨ Kitchen
⑩ Office
⑪ Wine bar
⑫ Food preparation
⑬ Staff wardrobe and toilet
⑭ Sprinkler
⑮ Dessert preparation
⑯ Rooms
⑰ Staff / service spaces
⑱ Installation spaces
⑲ Roof terrace

(Before)

(After)

Attic plan

a luxurious focal point of the city. Traditional, authentic historical appearance was maintained in the exterior, while the new interior designed by Studio Franić Šekoranja with 3LHD is visually lavish, eclectic, modern, classic, and elegant, with an abundance of texture, shades, and colors. When designing the interior concept, the emphasis was placed on creating the atmosphere and aesthetics rather than the restoration of the original interior. The main characteristic of the interior is the site-specific art installations, complemented with smaller works that are placed throughout the space, whose creators are well-known international artists. The entire hotel art collection consists of more than a hundred pieces of museum value.

The artists and art pieces were selected by curator Vanja Žanko. The artists used various media and were united on the project by an active wish for a deeper connection with the space and its heritage value. The creation of site-specific artworks required a constant fine-tuning and testing of their own practice from the artists, and the work on this hotel represented a true collaborative challenge for all of the participants.

Hotel One Shot Fortuny 07

Location / Madrid, Spain

Completion / 2017

Area / 42,141 square feet (3,915 square meters)

Client / One Shot Hotels

Design / Alfaro-Manrique Atelier

Photography / Victor Sajara, Creativersion

Alfaro-Manrique Atelier is made up of a team led by architect Gema Alfaro and industrial designer and architect Emili Manrique. Gema Alfaro has a Masters in International Project Management and has been working in architecture and interior design in the hotel sector since 2005. Emili Manrique teaches at the University of Juan Carlos I in Madrid and is completing his doctoral thesis on tourism and the hotel sector.

○ The space

The new One Shot Fortuny 07 Hotel is surrounded by buildings that go back to the nineteenth century, giving the area a characteristic look. The building in which the hotel is found was built in 1913 with a huge interior patio and a façade with an eclectic character to it, and is rich in shapes with historical resonance. In the interior all those elements were kept and integrated into the final project as part of the building's essence. Some of these elements included the main staircase, built fully in wood with a base covered with classical Andalusian ceramics; and the entry hallway with its wooden ceiling beams.

The interior design created by Alfaro-Manrique alludes to this history at the same time as it evokes a new design language of clear geometric forms.

○ **The flow**

In the route taken by the visitor from the streets to the most intimate space, the room, each space refers to the next at the same time as it recalls the previous one.

(Before)

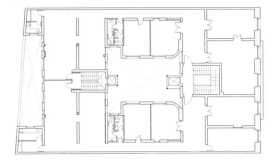

(After)

Second-floor plan

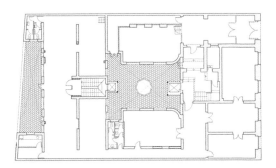

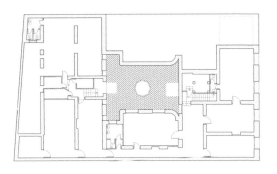

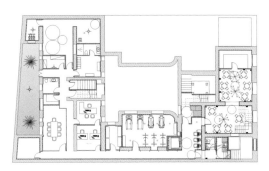

First-floor plan

Basement plan

(Before)   (After)

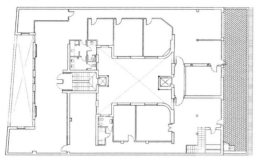 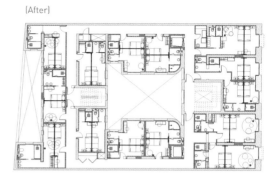

Attic plan

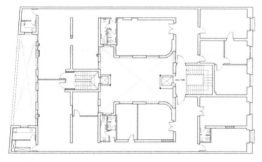 

Fourth-floor plan

Third-floor plan

○ **Decoration**

The same geometric language is used in all the different scales, from the smallest elements, such as the trays in the bathroom, to the vertical elements that create the lobby space.

A variety of materials are used, including black marbles from Marquina, white Carrara marbles, brass metals, natural woods, and an extensive range of different coated finishes, creating a unique surrounding which balances new elements with the memory of the past.

The textiles used for the sofas and chairs have been mainly velvets, which give the space a sensation of warmth and richness. Carpets, sofas, and footrests have been specially designed for this hotel in a rich variety of unusual shapes and a heterogeneous color palette that matches the chromatic richness of the interior.

○ Design elements

The color treatment has been used as the axis around which the complete interior scenery generated for the hotel is designed. The colors have been used for the coatings in the different elements that have been designed, such as wardrobes, desks, tapestries, carpets, and doors. They offer a vivid and fresh touch to the scenery and at the same time reference the color palette used by painters such as Goya. The main reference used for the color palette of the hotel was one of Goya's most famous drawings, from a compilation called "Cartones para Tapices."

The lighting, designed specifically for this hotel, starts in the lobby space with a huge light suspended at the top of the stairs, and then starts transforming gradually into new geometric shapes.

The hotel is accessed through a gardened hallway in which elements start to appear, such as modules, luminary elements, and even a bust of Leocadia, Goya's last wife, reinterpreted as a contemporary work of art. These elements act as a guide to what will be found in the interior of the hotel. The garden is reproduced again in the interior patio, where an orchard has been introduced.

Long Story Short Hostel

Location / Olomouc, Czech Republic

Completion / 2017

Area / 10,763.9 square feet (1,000 square meters)

Client / Long Story Short

Design / Denisa Strmiskova Studio

Photography / Josef Kubicek

Thanks to her MA scenography education at the Academy of Performing Arts in Prague, Denisa likes to work with the narrative and metaphorical approach in her projects. At the same time, her work is based on the nature of the specific situations in which she finds pure creative solutions.

She composes the atmosphere of space, looks for stories and creates new experiences. She does not work as a classical architect. With her insight she intuitively works with her feelings and emotions, friendly communication with the clients and finding what every project needs.

Her recent work includes the interiors of cafés, hostels, and other public areas or scenography of exhibition installations and storefronts. She has, however, no limits and is open to new challenges every time.

○ The space

The hostel currently offers accommodation in several private and dorm rooms, with 56 beds altogether. The private rooms offer comfort with a private bathroom. Bigger dorm rooms, which include an original layout of sleeping zones, do not include private bathroom, but this is compensated for by the well-equipped shared bathrooms. The reception, which is simultaneously a common room and a café, is the heart of the hostel. The whole concept of the hostel was created from scratch, including all its equipment and visual layout. The main idea was to highlight the historical spirit and with appropriate adjustments to enrich it with contemporary design. An organically arched hall, which leads from the reception to all the rooms, is different from every perspective and surprises the visitor constantly when walking through.

(Before)

(Before)   (After)

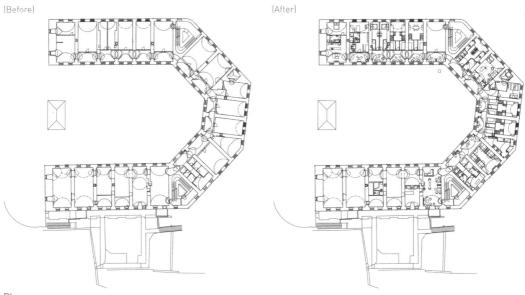

Plan

The whole concept creates a space where visitors feel comfortable. It also brings an aesthetic statement on the one hand, and functional scheme on the other. The designer's aim was to bring light to the interior, both inconspicuously and functionally. Simple lines of soft light straps were selected, providing lighting to the planes and intensifying the different vaulting of the corridors. This form of lighting preserves the clearances of spaces and minimizes the use of any larger elements that would disturb the layout.

○ **The flow**

The division of the space is determined by the historical character of the building and its original U-shape plan. The core part of the space is the reception which is connected with the café and open-air terrace. Reception contains leisure, information, and a meeting area. After checking in at the reception, the hostel guests enter the long U-shaped corridor which also offers seating to have a chat or just to relax below the historical arches. The way to all the dorms and shared bathrooms is via the corridor.

○ **Decoration and design elements**

Located in the historical centre of Olomouc, Long Story Short is set in a seventeenth-century brick building. Blending the original history of the building with a contemporary touch, the designer used raw materials like wood, stone, and metal. To soften things up a bit, she matched artwork from local craftsmen with delicate vintage furniture. Most of the furnishing is custom made. Beds, mirrors, lamps, shelves, as well as the bathroom equipment, were made to measure in cooperation with local producers.

The hall's shape is enhanced by the inconspicuous but still sophisticated use of light, for which the designer was inspired in scenography. Pure white plastering is in contrast with the black details as well as the carefully chosen pastel colors, which were used for upholstery of the sitting furniture arranged into intimate areas. All of this is elegantly combined with old modernist design of the previous century. The designer used small details (such as rotating light switches from the 1930s, black faucets, or the use of the hostel logo in unexpected places) to create a pleasant and perhaps surprising experience for visitors.

The Prestige Hotel

Location / Penang, Malaysia

Completion / 2019

Area / 92,247 square feet (8,570 square meters)

Client / The Prestige Hotel

Design / Ministry of Design

Photography / Edward Hendricks

Ministry of Design (MOD) is an integrated architectural, interior design, and branding firm that has won Singapore's President's Design Award twice, and New York's Gold Key Award three times. It was named Designer of the Year by International Design Awards (USA), and has been featured in *Wallpaper, Frame* and *Surface*. Created by Colin Seah to question convention and redefine the spaces, forms, and experiences that surround us, MOD's explorations are created amid a democratic studio-like atmosphere and progress seamlessly between form, site, object, and space.

○ The space

Located along Church Street in Penang, within the core zone of the George Town UNESCO World Heritage site, The Prestige Hotel is a new-build, joining many beautiful and intricate Victorian buildings that still house banking and commercial facilities, in a tropical climate where lush vegetation abounds.

The first-floor layout includes the reception, The Glasshouse restaurant, and retail spaces (such as San Francisco Coffee, a fine-dining restaurant, a local clothing brand, a dessert café, a florist, and a pharmacy) that are designed as standalone stores, providing a shop-in-shop concept to break down the linear scale, resulting in a check-in, eating, and shopping area reminiscent of the historical English shopping arcade.

There are four room types in total: the Deluxe, the Premier Deluxe suite, the Loft suite (designed for travelers on longer business trips or couples, this suite features a generous lounge on the first floor and a separate bedroom area on the mezzanine level), and a unique Deluxe Trio room which features a smaller bedroom for a child traveling with parents, for additional privacy. Besides featuring hidden pantries that are revealed behind the wainscot wall, the Loft Suite also features a custom-designed clock at the sofa area, which doubles up as a wall feature, making a fractal pattern out of the angular wainscot lines.

Taking the lift to the room levels, two and three, and to the event spaces on level four, is a confluence of modern Victoriana layered with local botany. The lift lobby surprises with a champagne bronze–tinted feature wall with etched patterning inspired by Victorian grilles and a window portal that frames the lush plants outside.

The top floor, level five, houses a fully equipped gym, amid chandeliers and mirrored ceiling panels to create the optical illusion of infinite space, and a generous events area. Named after the lead characters in the movie *The Prestige*, the Angier & Borden function rooms can host indoor events for 110 guests, and the Olivia and Julia outdoor gazebos feature lounge settings. The Angier & Borden function rooms feature mullions with fluted glass, providing privacy while maintaining light and porosity.

1. Entrance
2. WC
3. Safe
4. Minibar
5. Vanity
6. Shower
7. Wardrobe
8. Lounge area
9. Stairs to mezzanine
10. King bed
11. Single bed

Loft suite room plan

 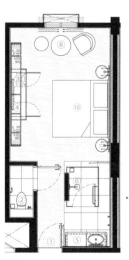 

Deluxe Trio room plan

Deluxe room plan

Premier Deluxe room plan

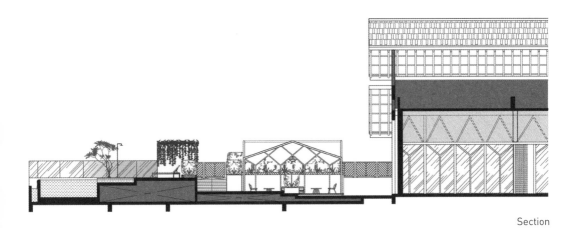

Section

○ **The flow**

One challenge the team faced was how to prevent a monotonous experience navigating through the hotel's long and narrow corridor. To overcome this, the studio introduced elements of visual trickery and surprise, notions of magic and illusions, with the end goal of creating delightful spaces and memorable guest experiences.

For example, the studio alternated dark and light color schemes along the guest-room corridors, to break down the potential monotony of the corridor experience. Mechanized light features were placed at regular intervals, to rotate and cast shadows of intricate lattice patterns to animate the guest journey. This visual animation and trickery ("smoke and mirrors") was borne out of a response to the unusual specificity of the long, narrow site, and is subtly introduced throughout the 162-room hotel.

○ Decoration and design elements

The colonial Victorian heritage and tropics are key elements of the design concept.

In the Glasshouse restaurant, taking inspiration from the English Victorian conservatory, the team applied a lattice pattern to the metal-framed walls

Fifth-floor plan

Third- and fourth-floor plan

Second-floor plan

①	Carpark	⑦	Gym
②	Lift lobbies (east and west)	⑧	Public washrooms
③	Back of house	⑨	Olivia gazebos
④	Guest rooms	⑩	Julia gazebos
⑤	Guest corridor	⑪	Pool deck
⑥	Function room	⑫	Pool

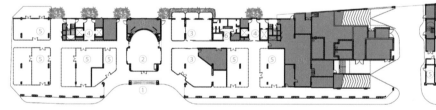

First-floor plan

①	Drop-off	⑤	Retail shops
②	Hotel reception	⑥	Public washrooms
③	All-day dining (The Glasshouse)	⑦	Bicycle park
④	Lift lobbies (east and west)	⑧	Back of house

(Before)

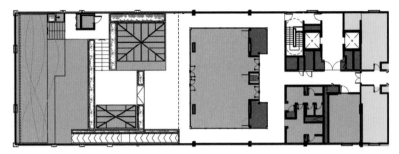

(After)

1. Lift lobby
2. Guest-room corridor
3. Gym
4. Public washroom
5. Function room
6. Lounge area
7. Olivia
8. Julia
9. Pool deck
10. Pool
11. Outdoor shower
12. Guest room

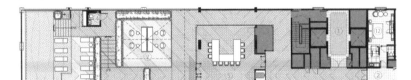

Public space plan

(Before)

Hotel lobby and The Glasshouse plan

(After)

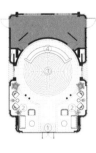
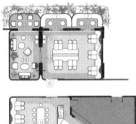

1. Main entrance
2. Lounge seating
3. Maze floor pattern
4. Reception desk
5. Back of house
6. Entrance
7. Banquette seating
8. Communal light table
9. Service station
10. Bar
11. Coffee machine
12. Kitchen
13. Indoor air-conditioned lounge
14. Indoor non air-conditioned lounge
15. Alfresco lounge

and glazing of the restaurant, presenting it as a garden conservatory for breakfasts, lunches, and dinners. In the guest rooms, the modern take on Victorian wainscoting was to craft angular trapezium-shaped lines, which provide a contemporized backdrop for the room.

In the reception area, designers introduced several tongue-in-cheek references to magical illusion, where guests navigate a custom-designed white marble-clad maze with brass trimmings on the floor, to get to the reception. The custom reception desk, made of mirrored stainless steel, magically appears to balance on chrome spheres, and a cloud wainscot adorns the curved wall behind the reception desk, showing a modern whimsical take on Victorian interiors. Other subtle visual trickery and surprises in the guest rooms include beds that seem to levitate and hidden doors that reveal toilet cubicles and hidden pantries.

In the guest rooms, a key feature in the Premier Deluxe suite is the custom-designed shower and wardrobe enclosure, crafted with champagne bronze–tinted metal and glass; a piece that takes aesthetic cues from the elaborate magic props used in performances such as Houdini's escape box.

Another custom-design piece is the vanity mirror frame. Abstracted from Victorian mirrors (usually heavy and elaborate) and modernized with its angular form, polished brass, and integrated light, this feature plays on optical illusions and perceptions, appearing as two mirrors but floating as a frame on top of a horizontal mirror wall.

In the lift car, the studio custom-designed a floor-to-ceiling polished tinted metal wall, graphically presenting the unique features of Penang in an aesthetic that is reminiscent of Victorian-like wallpaper. The graphic pattern comprises etched outlines of heritage buildings, famous landmarks (such as the clock tower and statues), and the local botany of Penang (coconut trees, birds of paradise, hibiscus, and Pinang palm trees).

Galeria Melissa NYC

Location / Soho, New York, United States

Completion / 2017

Area / 3,660 square feet (340 square meters)

Client / Galeria Melissa

Design / Muti Randolph

Photography / Alex Fradkin

Brazilian Muti Randolph is a pioneer in the use of computers as a tool for the visual arts. From virtual three-dimensional to real three-dimensional spaces, he creates graphics, illustrations, sets, and architecture projects mainly in the entertainment, fashion, and technology areas. In his installations and events, he explores the relation of time and space through music using custom-designed software and hardware. Projects such as D-Edge (São Paulo), Galeria Melissa (São Paulo, London, New York), Tube (São Paulo), Deep Screen (New York, Beijing), and the Sahara tent at Coachella 2011 (California), have been featured in architecture and design publications worldwide. He designed the Beyond Vision segment of the opening ceremony of the Rio 2016 Summer Paralympics.

○ The space

The space, which was originally a single open room, was divided into four main areas. The idea of the first space is to impact and attract visitors. It is a very striking passage for entering and exiting the boutique shoe store. The second space is the main product display and shopping area. From there customers can access the second art space and the lounge where the cash desk is located.

○ Dividing the space

The space division is in part based on the general concept for the Galeria Melissa boutiques that the designer first proposed for the São Paulo store: a first impression with great impact and surprise, the main

1. Art installation area
2. Technical
3. Vortex pyramid
4. Multiple-use staff area
5. Main display and selling area
6. WC
7. Lounge

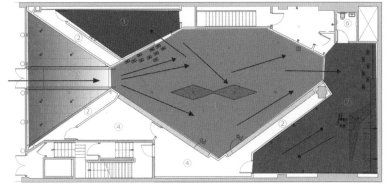

Functional areas and flow

exhibition area for temporary art, a main product display area, and a comfortable relaxing space at the end. But for the New York project the designer chose to play with the contrast of contemporary design and the iconic Soho cast-iron architecture, creating what he jokingly called "the clash of civilizations"—pyramidal spaces alongside Roman columns. The first pyramid is a kaleidoscopical LED and mirror vortex to "suck" people from the street into the main space, a double pyramid where the main shopping experience takes place. From there the customer can escape into a triangular art exhibition room, or relax in the lounge, which uses organic materials such as wood and live plants to offer relief from the previous high-tech and colder experience.

(Before)

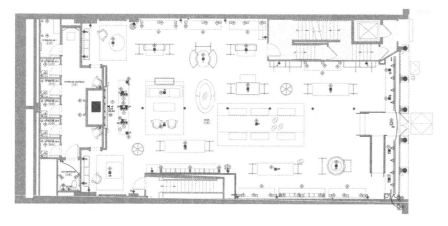

(After)

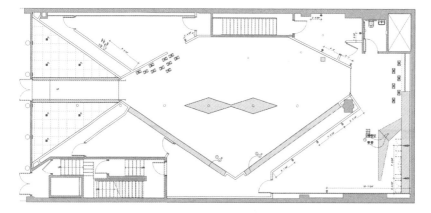

Floor plan

The dimensions of the spaces were determined having in mind the quantity of products to be displayed, the circulation, and the visual impact.

○ **Decoration**

The furnishing elements are mostly pyramidal tables and benches made of Corian, as well as the columns display that mimics the existing iron columns that are typical of the area.

○ **Design elements**

One of the main concepts of the galerias is the possibility to change completely over time. In São Paulo, the store changes every three months with a new collection and invited artist. In London and New York, the immersive LED installations at the entrance allow the change to happen continually.

In-Sight Concept Store

Location / Miami, United States

Completion / 2017

Area / 1,830 square feet (170 square meters)

Client / In-Sight

Design / OHLAB

Photography / Patricia Parinejad

OHLAB is an award-winning office devoted to urban analysis and cultural research of contemporary society through design, architectural practice, and urban strategy. OHLAB was selected by Dezeen magazine as one of the six best emerging interior design studios of 2018 and was described by the Chicago Atheneum as "one of Europe's most important emerging architects." The office, directed by Paloma Hernaiz and Jamie Oliver, was originally established in Shanghai and moved to Madrid, and currently its main office is in Palma de Mallorca where a team of 18 architects, interior designers, and building engineers work in a variety of projects.

○ The space

The concept store for In-sight is located in the shopping mall Brickell City Centre mall in Downtown Miami, one of the booming areas of the city. It is a commercial space for self-designed and multibrand clothing, accessories, and design objects.

The interior-design concept started with interpreting in a figurative and spatial way the binoculars, the logo of the brand composed of two interlaced circles, with the aim of creating a new design language for the brand. Using this shape, the designers placed 24 panels in parallel along the store. The result is a dynamic, changing, and vibrant tunnel that became the main space of the store, connecting to the other areas.

The gaps between the panels, variously spaced, host all the functional areas of the store: entrance and shop window at the beginning,

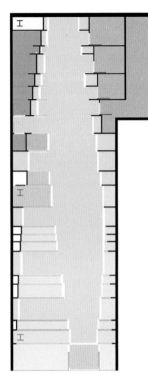

Functional areas

- Entrance
- Shop window
- Accessories display
- Clothing display
- Seating areas
- Counter
- Back office
- Fitting room
- Storage
- Distribution space

accessories display, clothing display, seating area, counter, back office, fitting room, and storage in closed rooms. Between the panels customers can see the products and the clothes exhibited, as well as sit and rest. Each of these functions is integrated in the overall design, thanks to the furniture, the material, and spatial relationships.

○ **The flow**

Despite the unusual shaped of the rounded panels, designers chose an archetypal circulation scheme with a main central gallery, the direction of which corresponds with the axis around which the frame panels move and rotate. Walking through this gallery, customers can access every side area, look at the items for sale, go deep into the corridor to see the clothes on display, or even stop and sit. More or less in the middle, located on one side, is the counter, which does not interrupt the circulation.

Every space, even the office and the storage, is linked together by the central corridor, a kind of floating fluid space that encourages people to cross and see the whole store, feeling free to continue the tour, to rest, or to linger.

○ **Dividing the space**

The simple parallelepiped space is divided by a series of parallel perforated panels, each unique in shape and designed to guarantee continuity and homogeneity to the space. The concept of the design is closely linked to the construction process of the panels.

Flow

Despite the formal complexity of the space, the construction system was simple and easy to dismount and mount again because all the panels were produced in a warehouse in Spain and shipped to Miami where the assembling took only a few weeks. The panels are built with a simple wooden structure finished with a very precise continuous edge of white Corian, easy to adapt to the curved geometry and resistant enough for the high traffic of a store.

No other element is placed to interrupt this spatial cohesion, and the auxiliary building structure is hidden behind it.

(Before)

(After)

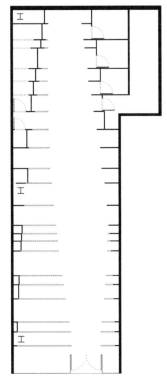

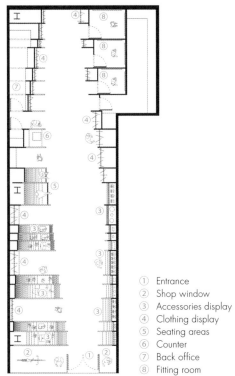

Floor plan

1 Entrance
2 Shop window
3 Accessories display
4 Clothing display
5 Seating areas
6 Counter
7 Back office
8 Fitting room

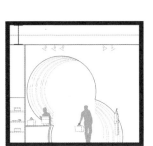

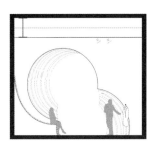

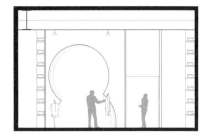

Sections

○ The dimensions

The main philosophy of OHLAB is to design for a specific use and space. The spatial concept allows us to create a fluid space but constantly split into little exhibition areas, each of which maintains a kind of cosiness despite being open. The distance of the white frames, and therefore the dimension of this area, is not accidental, but is calculated to offer a wide range of possibilities of use, including exhibition, sitting, and storage.

During the design phase the designers considered they wanted to catch the attention of customers not because of the quantity of exhibited elements, but rather by the quality of the space in which every product stands.

○ Decoration

The furnishing is integrated into the panels, using the same white color. A few volumes with sculptural shapes and clear lines, custom made for this shop, are placed between panels to be used as stands, seats, table, and clothes hangers. These simple geometries and the particular structure have been employed and interpreted to design an architectural language unique and respectful of the brand identity, made for this specific store.

○ Design elements

The space is an immersive experience, an interior tour through the ideas of In-sight. To increase the topological experience, designers decided to put at the end of the space a graphic panel that creates a trompe d'oeil illusion of continuity beyond the limits of the store.

As regards light, a key factor for any retail project, designers used a simple lighting system that takes advantages of the big panels, with a series of platforms with integrated swiveled spotlights directly supported on top of the frames. The spotlights are also very easy to move, adapting the light effortlessly to the changing exhibition of products in the center of the store.

BJK No1903

Location / Istanbul, Turkey

Completion / 2017

Area / 37,674 square feet (3,500 square meters)

Client / BJK Besiktas Construction and Trade Inc.

Design / Elips Design Architecture

Photography / Ali Bekman

Elips Design Architecture was founded in Istanbul in 1999, by architect Feza Okten Koca, and now comprises a team of architects, interior designers, and industrial designers. They produce projects especially in the fields of residential, commercial areas, food and beverage, retail, and education. Having started to produce furniture and lighting designs in this process, Elips Design Architecture decided to make these items under the brand of FEZA. In 2018, Elips' work on the BJK No1903 project won them three awards at the International Property Awards.

○ **The space**

This is a mixed-use commercial property named for a local football team founded in 1903. The lower basement floor houses the technical departments, while the first basement was for fitness, pool, and spa areas, and was provided with light from the front and rear façade with the level differences created in the field. On the first floor, the front-facing Casual restaurant and the rear-facing lounge area were located with their own terraces, while the main kitchen and service areas were placed close to the service entrance. The BOLD restaurant, with a large bar and fireplace area, is on the second floor, and moveable walls mean it can be combined with Blackhall, an events hall, if required. Facing the rear façade, the football club president's meeting room is located in a special section.

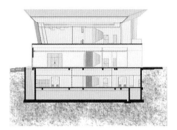
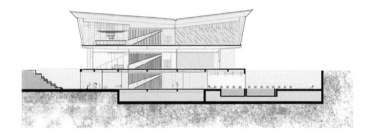

Sections

○ The flow

When designing a mixed-use project, it is necessary to plan an accurate flow while allowing different functions to take place in the spaces. The facility is accessed from the outside with two security entrances, one for the main entrance and one for the service entrance. The building's main entrance and the service entrance are provided from the first floor. The first-floor restaurant is accessible both from the building and from its own terrace. Access from first floor to other floors is provided by two elevators and stairs for fire escape. Fitness and spa area in the first basement can be accessed inside the building. The outdoor pool can be reached from the basement floor or from the first floor outside, if desired. On the second floor, it is possible to reach the BOLD restaurant, Blackhall hall, the club president's special section, restrooms, and terrace from the elevator hall.

(Before)

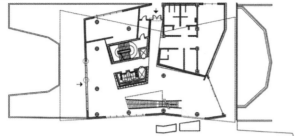

(After)

First-floor plan

(Before)

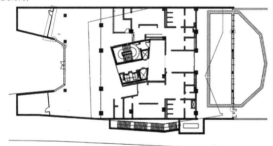

(After)

Basement plan

① Spinning
② Fitness
③ Functional room
④ Massage parlor
⑤ Men's changing room
⑥ Waiting hall
⑦ Women's changing room
⑧ Men's WC
⑨ Men's shower
⑩ Steam room
⑪ Sauna
⑫ Pool lobby
⑬ Women's WC
⑭ Women's shower
⑮ Indoor pool
⑯ Outdoor pool
⑰ Paddling pool
⑱ Back garden
⑲ Front garden
⑳ Café
㉑ Hall
㉒ Kitchen
㉓ Chef room
㉔ Cold room
㉕ Electrical room
㉖ Lounge
㉗ Seminar room
㉘ Restaurant
㉙ Cloakroom
㉚ Storage
㉛ Management's WC
㉜ Management's corridor
㉝ Management's meeting room

Designers aimed to increase the efficiency of functional areas by keeping the circulation areas to a minimum in the building. By providing a highly flexible design, they have provided multifunctional use of spaces.

(Before)

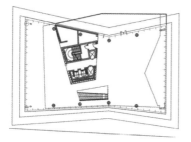

(After)

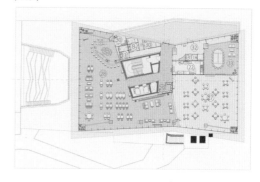

Second-floor plan

Generally, designers made the space divisions with gas concrete and iron construction plasterboard walls. They used glass separators and doors in some areas. Between Blackhall and BOLD, they used a movable wall to enable it to be combined when needed.

○ **Decoration**

The design agency designed and produced all the fixtures. In general, they used natural veneer wood and lacquered products, as well as marble, metal, and glass, and stainless and brass plating in some details. Darker colors were used in the BOLD restaurant, and more light and colorful designs in the Casual restaurant. Leather sofas were placed in the Lounge, while for Casual the designers tried to create a warm atmosphere with fabric-covered chairs and armchairs. On the fitness floor, they designed compact laminate-coating products for moisture resistance.

○ Design elements

Different lighting systems were used to create visual effects.
Circulation and service areas were illuminated by spots. Hidden
lights were placed between wall and ceiling connection lines. Barrisol
lighting was used on the Lounge ceiling, while in the Casual restaurant
square spotlights for general lighting, table lighting, and bar lighting
were provided with pendant products. Meeting-room lighting was
supported by a similar design with the camera visor in the middle of
the ceiling design and sconces on the walls. The BOLD restaurant
was illuminated by a pendant hanging from the high ceiling, as well as
lighting on the bar and drink stand. In the outdoor pool, hidden lights
on the floor and walls, and directional lights, were used to reveal trees
and plants.

Minneapolis Bouldering Project

Location / Minneapolis, United States

Completion / 2017

Area / 44,097 square feet (4,097 square meters)

Client / Minneapolis Bouldering Project

Design / Lilianne Steckel Interior Design

Photography / Andrea Calo

Lilianne Steckel studied interior design undergraduate at San Diego State University and graduate at Florence Design Academy. She moved to Austin, Texas in 2010 from Los Angeles and founded Lilianne Stechel Interior Design in early 2012. She designs for both residential and commercial spaces.

○ **The space**

The co-owners from Seattle Bouldering Project and Austin Bouldering Project came together to open a new bouldering facility, hoping to bring the concept to the northeastern region of the United States. They found the perfect site for it in Minneapolis, Minnesota.

The building, in an industrial complex lining the river, formerly housed an industrial office, manufacturing plant, and warehouse. Joining together two empty suites in the building, the Minneapolis Bouldering Project has 20,108 square feet (1,868 square meters) dedicated to climbing.

Designers removed some of the existing mezzanine areas from the original layout of the building to open up the possibility of full, two-story-height climbing areas in the central area of the space. These climbing walls can be viewed from almost every part of the gym.

The reception is at the entry with a retail display and check-in stations. Locker rooms reside in the center of the facility across from the central climbing areas.

The back of the gym offers special-use zones including child and teen climbing areas; a private birthday room; a workout classroom; cardio equipment area; and an open workout area.

The employee offices and lounge are in the back of the building tucked under the only remaining mezzanine. This mezzanine portion kept from

Yoga
Cubbies
Work
Meeting
Fitness
Teen
Kids
Birthday room
Hall and cubbies
Reception and card scan
Check-in and retail

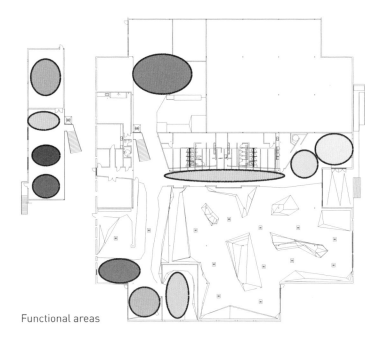

Functional areas

the original plan holds a flexible lounge for co-working and hangout area that overlooks the climbing walls. It also has a yoga studio and small yoga lounge tucked in the corner.

○ **The flow**

Designers saw the central channel of the building as a spine that gave an opportunity to branch the areas for special use out from it.

The only space where members come to a closed area in a corner of the building are special-use rooms and employee spaces. Otherwise, the

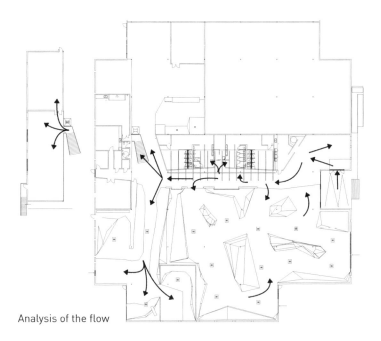

Analysis of the flow

designers tried to keep an open and intuitive route to where everything is located.

Designers were excited about making a social opportunity for the fitness community to gather, work out, hang out, shelter from the weather, have events, and motivate each other in a positive and thoughtful environment. They focused on each area as a new opportunity for a member to enjoy their experience at the gym, allowing different ways to use the gym based on the area they visit, the fitness activity they practice, and the type of mood they are in.

Designers wanted the space to feel open and filled with light. Each special-use area has its own specific needs and level of noise. They tried to keep the quiet and private areas closed off and the rest of the areas open to one another.

The child and teen areas are grouped together and separated for ease of supervision, and the workout areas are grouped together to ensure the age requirement is easily observed.

(Before)

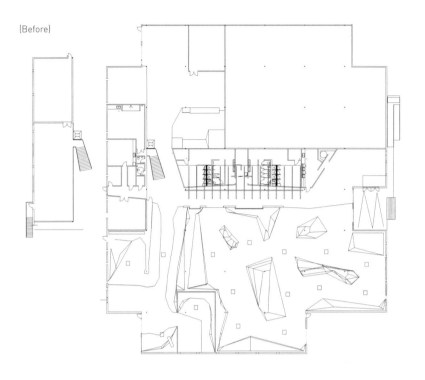

(After)

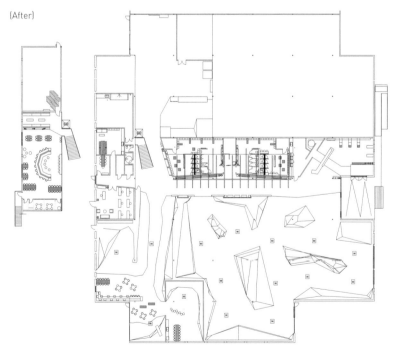

Floor plan

Painted steel signage with laser-cut letters marks each new zone as members approach it.

Designers created lounge cubbies where members can read, benches and banquettes where they can wait for friends, and active chairs and stools for those days when you have energy to spare. Cubbies and coat racks are located in each area to allow quick storage options outside of the lockers in the locker room.

Designers wanted the footprint of the climbing walls to be as large as possible, but made sure to allow enough space for back of house, employee areas, storage, and lounge areas.

○ **Decoration**

Lilianne Steckel wanted to create a bouldering environment unique to Minneapolis that blended the inherent industrial bones with an energetic and inviting space that felt synced to the active community.

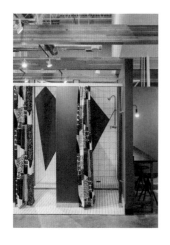

It is a location appealing to seasoned climbers and beginners, teens, adults, and families—a warm and open space accessible year-round for fun and fitness.

The long custom-made reception desk has a hand-painted mural towering behind it. A Dekton counter folds over the desk edge with a custom geo-shaped lighting fixture and to the right, a retail display area staggers wood and steel tables with perforated steel spines. The center corridor of the gym allows passage between the climbing walls and the locker rooms with glulam laminated timber beams overhead and clear panels filtering light into the locker rooms. Locker rooms hold saunas and showcase custom tiles in geometric designs in the showers, Pottok wallpaper, and fir-clad entry walls.

In the teen climbing and seating area, designers made stadium stairs with cubby pull-outs that are multipurpose as cubbies themselves and as tables for snacks or homework. The mezzanine is the main flexible area for co-working, gathering, and relaxing. It provides different seating opportunities like a faceted center banquette lounge with a work counter on the back side. Small group tables and lounge chairs fill the rest of the area, encouraging individual and group work, as well as lounging.

The overall aesthetic is a natural and bright palette with special energetic moments mixed in, allowing for high traffic and durability, but staying modern and encouraging the visiting members to lounge as well as use the gym for fitness. Designers used natural wood, treated concrete, painted steel, wallpaper, and pops of colors in custom upholstery and murals.

○ **Design elements**

The dramatic window-scape of the building façade gives a glimpse inside, instantly drawing people into the activity of the main climbing zone and reception. A colorful, custom wall mural by local artists, Impulse Creative, greets members upon entry.

Designers worked with Impulse Creative on creating pattern, texture, colors, and layout of the mural. They hand-painted it, creating patterns inside shapes on the spot and playing with fading color opportunities. They wanted the vibrancy and energy to welcome people into the space. Pottok designed and made the wallpaper featured in the restroom and locker room. Custom paint patterns were created in the teen and yoga areas to add personality to them.

Since the weather in Minneapolis is known for being harsh most of the year, designers wanted to have an indoor environment that was cheerful and natural, with murals and playful patterns that didn't overwhelm the members on the large expansive walls. For the main climbing areas, they chose a blue that would look inviting all year round, from morning light into night. The volume colors were then chosen to complement the blue.

The V Golf Club

Location / Vilnius, Republic of Lithuania

Completion / 2017

Area / 8,181 square feet (760 square meters)

Client / Vilnius Grand Resort

Design / PO NA MA

Photography / Darius Petrulaitis

PO NA MA is an architectural studio based in Vilnius, Lithuania. Founded in 2013, the studio has a young but experienced team of architects and designers, working on architectural and interior projects different in scale and typology.

○ **The space**

An old building at the Vilnius Grand Resort was reconstructed to become the V Golf Club, situated on a picturesque lakeshore and in the well-kept landscape of one of the most popular golf courses in the Baltic States. The project involved the replacement of existing facilities with a new range of hospitality offerings and functional spaces, and finding new connections between existing functions, such as the driving range and practice green, to make the club the center of a multifunctional golf course.

The single-story clubhouse contains areas for all aspects of socializing and golf-related activities. In addition to locker rooms, studio, pro shop, and supporting spaces, the building contains a restaurant with lounge area that is open to the public as well as club members.

The building's functional layout is structured by areas integrating outdoor activities and the clubhouse's interior functions together. The reception desk divides the flows to changing rooms, to practice green, driving range, pro shop, and restaurant with lounge. The restaurant is a large open space featuring several seating types arranged around a bar and fire pit. The building also houses the kitchen, administrative offices, and mechanical rooms.

The goal was to establish a unique connection with nature by capturing the elemental, vibrant beauty of the landscape. The structure helps to incorporate the environment into the interior space and find the harmony between the building, its interior, and its surroundings.

Almost all functional areas are connected with outside spaces—you can reach the practice green from the reception area; the restaurant opens up into a covered terrace; and the covered driving range is accessible from the building.

○ **The flow**

The clubhouse merges with the landscape and integrates consistently into the natural surroundings. The interior space is designed as a seamless transition into the golf course and becomes one with the

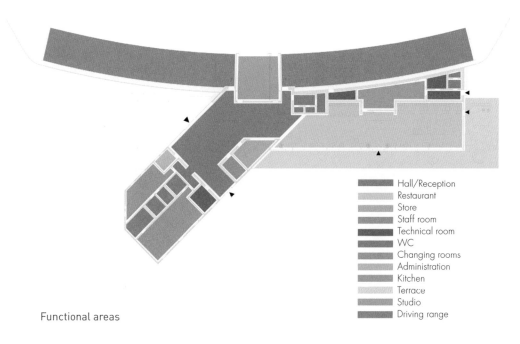

Functional areas

Hall/Reception
Restaurant
Store
Staff room
Technical room
WC
Changing rooms
Administration
Kitchen
Terrace
Studio
Driving range

surrounding. The open structure offers possibilities for multifunctional activities in one space, and serves as a location for golf or other events and award ceremonies. The clubhouse has become a lively place to socialize before, during, and after the game, and for public events. It provides spaces for recreational and cultural events both inside and outside, so there is close relationship between the landscape with outdoor activities and the club's interior program.

○ **Dividing the space**

One of the main goals of the design was to dissolve the limits between the landscape, the building, and the user. The simplicity of the linear

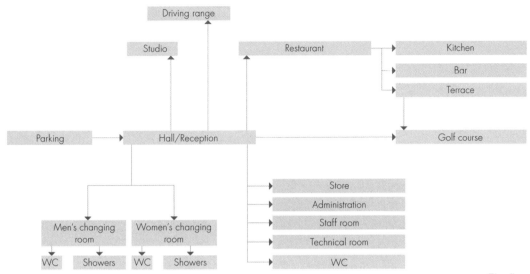

```
                    Driving range
                  ┌──────────────┐
                  │              │
        ┌──────────┐        ┌──────────┐      ┌──────────┐
        │  Studio  │        │Restaurant│─────▶│  Kitchen │
        └──────────┘        └──────────┘  ├──▶└──────────┘
                                          │   ┌──────────┐
                                          ├──▶│    Bar   │
                                          │   └──────────┘
                                          └──▶┌──────────┐
                                              │  Terrace │
                                              └──────────┘
┌──────────┐    ┌──────────────┐              ┌──────────┐
│  Parking │───▶│ Hall/Reception│────────────▶│Golf course│
└──────────┘    └──────────────┘              └──────────┘
```

Store
Administration
Staff room
Technical room
WC

Men's changing room
Women's changing room
WC   Showers   WC   Showers

The flow

plan enabled the team to structure spaces without any corridors. The clubhouse is an open, dynamic structure without clear visual limits. In such a way the space becomes liquid. There are several stable structures in the interior—the reception desk, restaurant bar, and fire pit. Around these space-division elements other functional zones are created. At the main entrance the reception desk divides the flow of people to the changing rooms, to the practice green, or to the lounge and restaurant area. At the restaurant area the fire pit divides the lounge area and seating zone. The designers wanted to divide the space into zones with the help of interior elements like furniture and interior details rather than walls. This enables space to be easily transformed according to individual customer need by modifying furniture layout.

The combination of solid walls and full-height glass walls to the lake and green delivers a relatively closed and framing visual effect and the feeling of openness and lightness, and also connects the interior seamlessly with the outdoors.

○ Decoration

Almost all furniture items were individually designed and produced by local craftspeople at the site. The furnishing design is ascetic and simple, yet comfortable and practical. Clear lines, simple volumes, and natural finishes were used to continue the main vision of the design—not to visually compete with the natural beauty outside.

(Before)

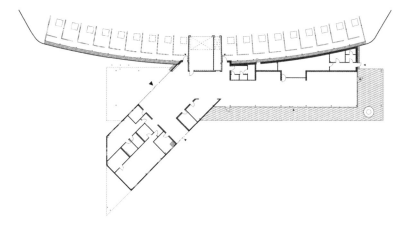

(After)

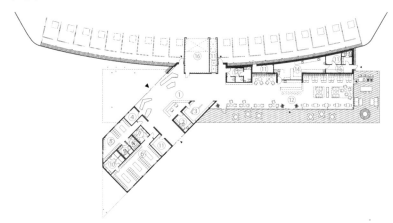

① Hall/Reception
② Staff room
③ Store
④ Administration
⑤ Women's changing room
⑥ Men's changing room
⑦ Men's WC
⑧ Women's WC
⑨ Women's shower room
⑩ Men's shower room
⑪ Technical room
⑫ Restaurant
⑬ WC
⑭ Restaurant kitchen
⑮ Corridor
⑯ Studio

Some furniture was designed as architectural elements, using façade materials. The warmth and texture of the wood is felt in the interior throughout the building. Dark, deep, solid colors contrast with the natural materials such as metal and hardwood, and stone and concrete emphasize the roughness of finishing.

○ **Design elements**

Horizontal elements emphasize the strict horizontal character of the building. Large showcase windows overlooking the rolling hills and natural lakes are at the center of the interior. Light is obtained by

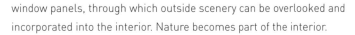

window panels, through which outside scenery can be overlooked and incorporated into the interior. Nature becomes part of the interior.

Natural materials like metal, concrete, wood, and stone were used. The materials used in façades and interior décor highlight the simplicity of the shapes. Concrete, hardwood, glass, and granite tiles are associated with naturally rough aesthetics, which creates a unique relationship with the surrounding.

Outdoor granite paving tiles are used inside the building, and the exterior and interior walls of the façade have the same finishing. Textured concrete is repeated in the interior on the floor. Roofs and ceilings are covered with the same materials both inside and outside which results in a solid slab effect.

The design tries to minimize the use of distinctive décor and colors, and maximize the impact of natural surroundings as the main accent by using bold, solid surfaces, and minimalist patterns.

These visual effects create a strong identity for the development, while not competing with the visually generous site.

Index